TIPS FROM ADVICE FOR STARTING A SUCCESSFUL SMALL OR MID-SIZE BUSINESS FROM THOSE WHO'VE DONE IT

©2022 Allen E Fishman

© Allen E. Fishman 2022

Direct Communication Services, Inc.
11031 Sheridan Blvd.
Westminster, CO 80020

Table of Contents

DEDICATION.. i

ACKNOWLEDGEMENTS ii

PREFACE... iii

THE ALTERNATIVE BOARD (TAB) vii

INTRODUCTION.. 1

PART ONE: TYPICAL MOTIVATIONS AND
TRAITS OF SUCCESSFUL BUSINESS FOUNDERS. 5

  CHAPTER ONE: MOTIVATIONS FOR STARTING
  BUSINESSES 6
  CHAPTER TWO: SBF TRAITS 17

PART TWO: LEARNING FROM SBF MISTAKES . 45

  CHAPTER THREE-MISTAKES MADE BY SEVERAL
  SBFs.. 46
  CHAPTER FOUR-MISTAKES MADE BY ONE OR A
  FEW SBFs 67

PART THREE: YOUR SELF DISCOVERY.............. 76

  CHAPTER FIVE: SWOT EVALUATION 77
  CHAPTER SIX: PERSONAL VISION STATEMENT
  101
  CHAPTER SEVEN: WHY HAVE YOU FAILED TO
  START A BUSINESS? 113

PART FOUR- SELECTING THE BUSINESS TO
START THAT BEST FITS YOU 129

  CHAPTER EIGHT: SELECTING THE RIGHT
  BUSINESS FOR YOU TO START 130
  CHAPTER NINE: SELECTING A BUSINESS THAT
  WILL EMPLOY FAMILY MEMBERS 143

PART FIVE: SHOULD YOU START A BUSINESS BY BUYING A FRANCHISE? 150

CHAPTER TEN- PROS OF OWNING A FRANCHISE 151

CHAPTER ELEVEN- CONS OF OWNING A FRANCHISE 159

PART SIX: SELECTING THE RIGHT FRANCHISE FOR YOU 168

CHAPTER TWELVE: SEARCHING FOR A FRANCHISE THAT IS THE BEST FIT FOR YOU . 169

PART SEVEN: THINGS TO DO BEFORE BUSINESS OPENS WHEN STARTING A BUSINESS FROM SCRATCH 197

CHAPTER THIRTEEN: YOU 199

CHAPTER FOURTEEN: PRE-OPENING STRATEGIC PLANNING 204

PART EIGHT: OUTSIDE RESOURCES 234

CHAPTER FIFTEEN: FINANCING RESOURCES . 235

CHAPTER SIXTEEN: OTHER OUTSIDE RESOURCES 255

CONCLUSION 263

DEDICATION

Judi, I met you for the first time when you were 16 and I was 18. I loved the sound of your voice and your smile from the moment I met you. Your love and support have been so important in making my life an incredible journey.

ACKNOWLEDGEMENTS

Thanks to those business founders who own successful businesses worldwide and generously shared their advice with me. The great majority of those business owners are members of The Alternative Board (TAB). I refer to these successful business founders as SBFs in the book. They have shared what was needed to make their businesses successful and the mistakes they made that you should avoid.

PREFACE

My passion for business began in my early teens. It led me first to an undergraduate degree in finance and accounting. Then, it inspired me to earn a law degree.

Now, please forgive what will sound like bragging, but by the time I turned 26, I was already the Vice President of a division of a multibillion-dollar Fortune 500 public company. Happy as I was about achieving that position so early in my career, I still had a nagging feeling that something was missing.

What was missing was the fulfillment that comes with owning and running a business. Missing was the satisfaction of *controlling my destiny*. The void my title and its accompanying responsibilities couldn't fill what was missing.

So, three years later, I surprised (and worried) family other than my wife Judi, friends, and colleagues by leaving the Vice President position, sizeable paycheck, and pre-ordained career path behind. In their place, I accepted a court appointment to become the Receiver of a company that had gone bankrupt.

Why I would opt to spend my days pumping the life back into a bankrupt company mystified my inner circle. But my instincts proved to be correct. Rehabilitating a fallen enterprise was the fastest possible path to getting hands-on experience leading a business.

By the time the Receivership ended, I felt ready to invest in a company. I became co-owner of Tipton, a small consumer electronics and appliance chain with stores in or around St. Louis, Missouri. My experience at Tipton and the company's expansion were incredible. At one point, Tipton ranked 54th in growth among privately-owned companies in the United States.

After achieving record-breaking profits, we took Tipton public, and Tipton was later acquired by a much larger publicly owned company. Shortly after the sale, I resigned as company President and moved to the Aspen, Colorado area.

At that time, I knew that I loved the business world but didn't plan to get involved again in running a company. My compromise with myself was to do a few different business-related activities.

I wrote a weekly business column that included answering business-related questions from readers, which was nationally syndicated throughout the USA. I hosted a weekly radio segment that was nationally syndicated in the USA. And I also gave speaking engagements around the country, sharing business advice.

After a few years, I realized that no amount of writing, radio programs, or speaking engagements would deliver the satisfaction of owning and building a business. But I did not attempt to start or buy a business because I was concerned that doing so would interfere with the new lifestyle I had come to enjoy. I loved my lifestyle, which included hiking, skiing, mountain biking, and playing tennis

Then, one night at a party where every couple included a business owner, I recognized a need that business owners had and a way to satisfy the need. The need was for affordable advice from other business owners. The answer I came up with was to create a system that I believed would help business owners worldwide.

Before I could move ahead in launching a new company, which I named The Alternative Board (TAB), I had to address the fact that launching TAB would mean that I had a new challenge: I felt zealous about managing my time, resources, and energy. Could I successfully launch a new company while maintaining the new lifestyle I had enjoyed after Tipton was sold? Could my vision for the business be achieved without me being at an office or available during regular business hours?

I decided that the work/life balance I wanted could be achieved, but I would need self-disciple to keep the balance. I would need to accept the reality that the new company would grow much slower than it could if I fully dedicated myself to be available during regular business hours.

So, I moved ahead with starting TAB, and the results have been incredible. TAB has helped tens of thousands of business owners worldwide lead their companies more successfully while enjoying their lives more. And that has generated the most fulfillment I've experienced in my career.

THE ALTERNATIVE BOARD (TAB)

TAB is a global membership organization of members who own small and midsize businesses. The members attend TAB monthly peer advisory board meetings along with a small group of other business owners that operate in business industries that do not compete with the other members on the board. We refer to the groups as *TAB Boards*.

The monthly TAB Board meetings, held in person or virtually, serve as confidential "think tanks." Members present challenges and opportunities on which they want advice. TAB Board meetings consist of up to 10 business owner members.

A TAB-certified Implementer facilitates the TAB Board meetings and also provides coaching. In addition, TAB Implementers offer other services to help their members. For example, they provide strategic planning services using TAB's *StratPro System*. They provide TAB's management development training programs and executive coaching for executives and other managers employed by the members. TAB-certified Implementers are franchisees trained by TAB to chair board meetings and coach TAB members.

In addition to TAB peer boards limited to members who own established businesses, TAB also has peer boards, called Accelerator Boards, exclusively for business owners whose businesses are in the first few years.

INTRODUCTION

Business ownership is where those with talent and drive can succeed regardless of gender, ethnicity, race, or religion. When I was very young, my father told me, "the only employer you don't have to worry about holding you back due to bias against you is the one you see in the mirror." In other words, the best way to avoid bias in the workplace is to become your own boss.

So, when you start your business, you will find that the company's success is up to you. You will do things your way and not feel that something isn't succeeding because of someone else. It's a great feeling to have.

The Path to This Book

I have a passion for helping others start businesses. I am often asked, "What's your interest in helping others start businesses, Allen?" It's a fair question. My interest in helping others start businesses began before I launched TAB.

For many years, I volunteered to help friends start enterprises that fulfilled their dreams of owning a business that became a successful small or midsize company. Through that experience, I developed a course for people considering entrepreneurship. The idea was to provide tools and guidance to help truly motivated people start their businesses *the right way*. It wasn't long before the course

1

began yielding results, assisting those who followed its principles to build successful businesses and lead rewarding lives.

Then, with advice shared by TAB members who started businesses that became very successful, the course material expanded over the years. And today, you are reading the result of that collaboration.

Unfortunately, the wisdom needed to start a business the right way is not something that rookie business owners have. But the insight from those who have done it is available and shared in this book. The tips, guidance, and recommendations drawn from these successful business founders ("SBFs"), along with my own experience and course material, morphed into this book.

This book is for everyone thinking about starting a business, including those in that group of would-be business owners who have difficulty taking the first step toward business ownership. Conversely, this book is also for those unsure if they should become business owners. It will help them recognize whether being an entrepreneur is right for them.

Getting Started

This book will make it easier for you by showing you how to get out of the starting gate and identify and eliminate wasted steps toward opening your new business. You will learn how to make things happen.

You will begin to grasp:

- Most of what is happening
- Why it's happening, or isn't
- What needs to happen next

One of my goals is to take the mystery and complexity out of the process. In simple, conversational language, I will explain how you can select and start the business that fits you best and becomes successful.

Not A One-Size-Fits-All

Starting a new business is not a one-size-fits-all scenario. For example, there's a big difference between starting a business with no employees (so-called "Solopreneurs") or only a few employees versus a company that relies on a sizeable staff. In this book, I will share what needs to be done differently according to the employee size of the business you wish to launch.

Take the Baton of Knowledge

Ask any business owner, and they will tell you: Nothing prepares you to know what it is like to own a business until you become a business owner. You can take endless courses on entrepreneurship; you can even earn an MBA. You won't know what it's like until you're on the field, moving the ball toward your goal.

But you can learn a significant amount from what others who have founded businesses, which I call SBFs, did that resulted in their start-up businesses becoming successful. It's also essential that you learn about the mistakes they made *so that you can avoid making* their mistakes. Steering clear of falling into the same potholes will help your companies succeed.

So, let's do it together! Shall we proceed?

PART ONE: TYPICAL MOTIVATIONS AND TRAITS OF SUCCESSFUL BUSINESS FOUNDERS

In this Part One, you will learn about some things that successful business founders have in common to determine whether you share these factors. This includes understanding what made the SBFs highly motivated to start their businesses. And the most common traits that they share are the willingness to commit to making the sacrifices necessary to succeed.

These motivations and traits significantly increased the odds of success for the new businesses started by these business founders who have developed successful companies (SBFs).

CHAPTER ONE: MOTIVATIONS FOR STARTING BUSINESSES

Everyone who took my course on starting a business likely had dreams of launching a company of their own. Why else would they have signed up? And yet, only about 25% of them followed through.

What happened to the other 75%? What may explain the 75% who bailed is that most people who consider starting a business never fully commit. What is the hardest part of doing anything? Getting started. That's especially true of launching a new business. They didn't get started toward starting a business in most cases. In short, you'll learn to overcome the obstacles that keep people from "wanting to start a business" versus "doing it!"

In this chapter, we will look at what inspired the 25% who proceeded. When I queried business owners who currently run successful businesses (SBFs), their typical answer was that they were highly motivated to start their businesses regardless of the type of business, the country in which it operates, or the background of its founder.

Most of them had more than one strong motivation. Although these SBFs started their businesses, their reasons differed because *the founders were driven to do it*. Many had more than one motivation pushing them to start their businesses. And when they become fully engaged, there is no stopping them. They make it happen, even knowing and accepting that most start-ups don't survive five years.

Below, I have separated into two groups these SBFs based on their motivating factors. The first group consists of SBFs with motivating factors important to at least 50% of the SBFs. The second includes SBFs with motivations that inspired at least 30% of the SBFs.

GROUP ONE

Motivational Factor #1: Desire to Earn More Income

As you would expect, the motivation for most of the SBFs to start their companies was to earn more income. They felt that their earning potential in their current jobs limited their chances of making the money they wanted. Reaching the level of financial success that they desired seemed unachievable while working for someone else.

They felt that they could earn the money they wanted by owning businesses. And the reality is that if companies are successful, their owners generally make far more than they would have earned as employees. In most countries, only a tiny percentage of people can retire at 65 and maintain the same standard of living they had before retiring. Most of them own or have owned businesses.

Motivational Factor #2: Enable Them to do What They Want to do with Their Lives

Most of the SBFs reported that making money alone was not what led them to start their new businesses. They said that their greatest motivation was it would lead them to be able to do *what they wanted to do with their lives.*

Money was a consideration, but it wasn't a motivation only for having wealth. While SBFs wanted their businesses to make money, they were more energized by their belief that it would allow them to be able to do things they enjoyed, and that made them happy. So, although making more money was one of the most common triggers for SBFs starting their businesses, creating wealth wasn't their greatest inspiration.

Motivational Factor #3: Self Value

For some of the SBFs, earnings were a way of keeping score. One SBF told me that making money affirmed his value in the same way that getting a good grade did at college. Many SBFs indicated they received more pleasure from making money than spending it because of how making money reflected upon them.

Some who mentioned getting satisfaction from their businesses' success referred to their companies as their "babies." These SBFs seem to view the achievements of their companies as status symbols for how others view them. They get an emotional high when their company succeeds.

Wishing to be viewed as a winner is a common trait of business owners. Most SBFs admit it was important that others viewed them as successes; they felt that being a business owner earned greater recognition and prestige than working for others. They wanted greater prestige or status in how others viewed them and saw this attained if they were owners of successful businesses. They felt that owning successful businesses would cultivate an image of being successful and that recognition would add value to their lives.

For many, being a business owner provides framing for their identity and self-worth. Their businesses' success and involvement are vital to their social presence.

Motivational Factor #4: Controlling Destiny as the Boss

It was common to hear from SBFs that they disliked being managed by others and decided that they would never be happy working for someone else, regardless of how much they made and how "rewarding" the positions were.

Before becoming business owners, many had positions with impressive titles, responsibilities, and compensation. They worked for good people who treated them well and paid them well. But ultimately, they were dissatisfied because they were working for someone else.

Their desire for independence and not having to take orders from someone else was more substantial than the "security" of the money they were making or their impressive titles. Even if it meant sacrificing for a while, they would rather be their bosses and prove they could succeed.

They viewed the potential rewards of owning a business as significant, both financially and emotionally. Even though most successfully worked as employees for others, the SBFs needed to be in charge to be happy. Nothing an employer could do would eliminate their feelings about working for someone else.

Motivational Factor #5: Lost Job

Some SBFs leaped to start a business to avoid being vulnerable again after being furloughed or laid off. Well, the fact is that a lifetime job in most companies is a rarity. Good employees often get fired for various reasons that have nothing to do with their performance. Some SBFs had dedicated 15 to 20 years to a career, only to find themselves out on their butts. The reasons for their being let go included their employing companies being sold, their employers downsizing, or a change in the executives to whom they reported.

They learned that seemingly secure jobs do not provide long-term job security. They decided they did not want to re-enter the job market. Why? Because they realize the next job may be even less secure than the previous one, and they want more control of their futures.

They realized that true job security only exists *when you own your job* and know that they had to leave the "employee nest" if they wanted not to be vulnerable to being let go for things out of their control. They decided they wouldn't have to worry about being fired by an employer as business owners. They don't have to worry that their jobs might be in the crosshairs if new owners take over or other reasons good employees find themselves out of their careers.

Only one employer will be dedicated to creating your job security. You.

A successful business provides job security only when *you own your job*! A business owner's position is not vulnerable to an employer downsizing, going public, having division layoffs, or even bad relationships with your boss.

Motivational Factor #6: Passion

Turning a passion into an enterprise is a solid motivator to become a business founder. Most successful SBFs started their businesses in areas that invigorated them because it involved their passion. That inspiration was one of the reasons their start-ups became so successful. This factor deserves elaboration.

Even when the intensity at work is extreme, passion is the antidote to burnout. When you are building a business that you're passionate about, the hard work in addressing the inevitable challenges doesn't wear you or stop you from overcoming the challenges.

To start a business that involves what the founder views as meaningful is a powerful motivation to start the business. I started TAB during a time when I saw myself as retired. But I saw a way I could start a business that involved my passion for helping business owners and those who wanted to become business owners and, at the same time, keeping my lifestyle. Pursuing this passion was the most significant motivator for me in starting TAB.

Owning a business that involves something important to the founder gives the owner a greater sense of purpose. One executive was fired because of a change in the ownership of the business. He decided to start a business because he didn't want to be vulnerable again to being out of a job.

He had enjoyed making home improvements for friends and himself. So, he started his remodeling business because "it's something I love to do and feel passionate about." He told me that he spent long hours in his company. So passionate was he about his business that he had to discipline himself not to work too hard.

Many start their businesses because they want to be involved in something that matters to them. When combined with other motivations, the passion for making the world a better place results in businesses being started. Think about the companies like Tesla Automotive, Beyond Meat, and Patagonia that integrated the objective of helping the environment into their missions.

GROUP TWO

At least 30% of the SBFs were motivated to start their businesses by the following motivational factors:

Motivational Factor #7: Dissatisfied with Their Job

These SBFs decided to leave their jobs because they wanted more fulfillment from their work experience. Their dissatisfaction with what they were doing at work or job dynamics was a significant motivating factor to start businesses. Sometimes this dissatisfaction came from their dislike of company politics and unwillingness to "play the game."

They described that, at times, they felt paralyzed to do what they thought should be done by them for the companies that employed them. They felt that, as business owners, they would be able to turn decisions into action, doing what they believe is best for their businesses. They would no longer have to do the politically correct or safe options even if they felt the options were wrong for the company.

When SBFs expressed that they started their businesses because they had been dissatisfied with their jobs, I asked them, "Are you generally happy being a business owner?" The great majority of them responded yes. In short, they found their work as a business owner to be more fulfilling.

Many SBFs have left their jobs because they wanted their work to bring them more joy and fulfillment from work. Although these SBFs didn't like working long hours for someone else, they willingly spent that time with their businesses.

One SBF, who was in her early 60s when she started her business, was unhappy in her executive position and so disliked some of her responsibilities that she just avoided doing them. She had become a disgruntled employee who often gave excuses for not getting work done.

At a certain point in their careers, some accomplished executives accustomed to working long hours experience "burnout." One SBF explained that although she had been paid well, she no longer enjoyed many of her tasks as an executive with a distributorship company. Her boredom with her job greatly affected the quality of her life. She explained she was tired of being miserable. So, she gave up her secure, highly compensated position to start her own business.

In addition to meeting your financial goals, owning a business can give you the sense of accomplishment you can't get working for others.

Motivational Factor #8: Held Back Because of Gender, Age, Nationality, Race, or Religion

Even though cultural norms are shifting, some SBFs started their businesses because they felt held back in their jobs because of their gender, age, nationality, race, or religious bias. They saw owning a company as the way to overcome limits because business owners have no "glass ceilings."

These SBFs could be summed up by saying that they felt that no matter what laws existed to protect them, there was an unfair and inappropriate factor limiting their opportunities at work. They thought they would no longer have career path concerns if they became business owners.

Conclusion

How motivated are you to start a business? If you're not highly motivated about starting a business, think once, twice, and three times before moving forward.

Most successful business owners now look forward to working most days because they are highly motivated. The people who resented working long hours for someone else acknowledged that they are currently happily working even longer hours on behalf of the businesses they started.

Interesting side note, most of the SBFs who reported suffering burnout as business owners acknowledged that they focused on chasing money versus pursuing their passions.

CHAPTER TWO: SBF TRAITS

So far, we've identified many common motivations for jumping into the business owner pool. So, you might think there are also common background characteristics to the SBFs themselves — consistent patterns to their experience, age, gender, family history or level, and type of education of the business founders. And you would be dead wrong.

It turns out there *is no ideal background for who starts a business*: no perfect degree, pedigree, family makeup, or even business experience. However, SBFs felt some character traits were essential to their businesses becoming successful, established companies.

The following are the 23 different character traits that our SBFs identified. Let's explore each individually.

1. **Embrace Change**
2. **Good Leader**
3. **Curious by Nature**
4. **People-Oriented**
5. **Mental Ability**
6. **Confidence**
7. **Ability To Effectively Wear Many Hats**
8. **Obsessive About Making the Business   Succeed**
9. **Comfortable Being the Final Decision Maker**
10. **Willing To Assume Risk**
11. **Focused**

12. **Persistence**

13. **Able To Handle Stress**

14. **Strategic Thinker**

15. **Ambitious**

16. **Willing to Sacrifice**

17. **Troubles with Time Management**

18. **Live Within Means**

19. **Self-Accountable**

20. **Do Not Befriend Their Employees**

21. **Accept the Need for Them to Handle Confrontations**

22. **Keep Emotions in Check**

23. **Analyze Before Acting**

Common Trait #1: Embrace Change

With companies that fail, needed adaption doesn't happen for businesses with owners who keep their heads in the sand and don't try to or cannot innovate. In contrast, about two-thirds of the SBFs responded that their ability to make innovative changes was vital to the success of their companies. Sometimes the start-ups became successful only after the leaders changed the original business model.

When you launch any business, your business priorities will be in flux. Assume that problems will occur, and it will be up to you to adapt and solve them. Your focus will need to pivot frequently to accommodate the adjustments that allow your start-up to survive and succeed. What's more, you must be able to make changes promptly.

Many SBFs shared how challenging things were after starting their businesses. The beginnings of companies are typically demanding. One reason is that the founder's envisioned business model often does not work as anticipated.

Business founders who can respond to changes in the business environment, which sometimes happen almost overnight, have a much greater chance of their businesses succeeding. If time is available before they need to make changes, they devise and test innovative solutions for anticipated challenges and trends.

If you make decisions only when you can find the perfect approach, your new business is unlikely to achieve its potential. Businesses owned by those who embrace change are more likely to adapt as needed. Put another way. They have a healthy attitude toward solving problems and making required changes. They make changes based on what they are experiencing versus locking into plans that don't suit the new realities.

Be honest with yourself regarding what is working and what is not. Own up, step up, and move forward. As you are probably your most demanding critic, you need to learn to accept your mistakes and see what you can do to offset them.

SBFs are typically agile because no matter how much research and planning you do before starting your new business, the path forward will not be a straight line. As a result, entrepreneurs need the urge to find answers to emerging problems and then make the required changes. When things veer from the path they had laid out, winning business owners adjust.

The need to adjust may even occur before you open the door for your new business. SBFs shared how they had to change their business models during the days leading up to the launch and the early days after their new companies started operating. Some had to adapt to market factors that they hadn't considered. Some had to streamline their operational processes to improve efficiency.

Many companies faced disappointments in their early years. Many refer to their first years as the "dark days." It is hard to make a start-up profitable. When there are challenges, don't make the mistake of putting your head in the ground to ignore what you may have underestimated as a challenge. No matter how well-thought-out your business plans are, your results may differ from what you projected. You will need to identify why the differences exist and make changes to correct the situation.

Most SBFs have had to adapt things, particularly during the first few years of operation, to make their businesses successful. Sometimes the needed changes are so extreme that they could be referred to as reboots. One SBF recounted the story of a very effective product handling what it intended to do. However, it had not sold well. Instead of giving up, he did a major "reboot," which included changing its name, packaging, marketing messaging, and target customers.

As for the product, he didn't make any changes to it because he believed in it. The result? The reboot transformed what was initially a failure into an incredibly profitable product that would become his company's primary driver of profits and high valuation when he sold the company.

But here's the critical ingredient. Business success is likely only to happen when the founders take the inevitable problems that crop up in their stride and focus on the needed adjustments. Your goal is to fix the negatives and focus on the positives, mainly if your business is stumbling through failures. You will typically need to create a plan or plans for your new business to overcome the hurdles for the fix to happen.

You will also need to make sure the plans are implemented. You must be committed to executing course changes that you think will work best for the business. Without proper execution, you are likely to have your changes fail.

After working for someone else as an executive or manager, many who start businesses need to break from the mindset that made them successful as corporate executives. They need to develop a trait of embracing change.

Opening your mind to *operating with flux, agility, and creative problem-solving* may be a different way to think about business planning and leadership. But you need to do it as the owner of a start-up business. When looking ahead, you need to learn from what happened in the past and make the necessary decisions.

Being able to see things in a different light can power the type of changes that have an essential impact on a company's success. Being creative won't bring about many benefits if there isn't the needed attention to making change happen. However, you can't make a change happen if you don't see the opportunity for the change. The creative vision must be communicated for the shift to occur so that employees will understand and support it. So, it's worth taking the time to make sure that the presentation for sharing the idea is done in a way that will most likely bring about understanding and support for the idea.

To reach the maximum potential for the success of your business, you need to be willing to learn and improve. That requires you to understand that you don't have all the answers. Sometimes you will need to revise your understanding of a problem you thought had already been solved. Be open to new points of view, information, ideas, contradictions, and challenges to your way of thinking.

Most SBFs are always looking for ways to improve what isn't working as well as it should. Many SBFs tried things that failed and learned from their errors. After receiving new input, they adapted.

The stage of business of your business may also bring about the need for change. For example, business plans labored over for months in year one of operation may need to be changed and improved as a business evolves.

Don't expect things for your start-up business to go precisely as you thought they would go. You will likely need course changes to make your new enterprise successful.

SBFs try to identify what is working and what is not after objectively looking at the available information. Once SBFs find the breakdowns, they make changes.

Of course, there is always more than one way to realize innovation in your new business! After all, innovation is simply creativity put to work for a purpose: One way to achieve innovation, schedule time each month for a brainstorming meeting of a creative think tank of employees dedicated to generating new business ideas. Another way is to offer bonuses for the best new ideas you put into operation.

Flexibility and adaptability are essential qualities for starting a business that will be successful. Change is the status quo if you want your company to succeed continuously. No matter how successful you may be, fight the instinct to maintain the status quo.

You don't have to be a natural innovator to start a business that becomes successful. But, without openness to change, your leap into entrepreneurship may have disastrous results. Don't start a business owner if you can't commit to making needed course corrections. Get advice from others if you recognize the need for change that the business requires (as most companies do) but do not know what the change should be.

To summarize, business owners must recognize needed changes and then take the required actions to implement them if they want their businesses to succeed. If you don't, your business will underperform or fail.

Also, if you could remember only one thing from this book, it's this: Don't let your mistakes stop you. You must be able to rebound from business defeats by creating and implementing course changes and doing them promptly so that your business can recover from business defeats.

Common Trait #2: Good Leader

Employees, particularly in a start-up, need to have confidence in you. Trust in your leadership ability is critical to running a successful business. Even though their leadership styles differed, most SBFs answered "yes" when

I asked if they felt they were good leaders of their companies.

Don't confuse, as some do, being a good communicator with being a good business leader. Some SBFs who felt very confident in their leadership ability acknowledged that they are poor communicators. This shows that you don't need to be an excellent communicator to be a good business leader. Other talents and skills can offset business founders' poor communication skills with their companies.

Ignoring problems is a way to lose confidence in your leadership quickly. One of the ways to bring about good communication is to learn from your employees by asking for and respecting feedback.

Business founders need to be honest and transparent with their employees regarding what works and what isn't. Give credit to who is responsible for things that are working. Openly discuss with your employees, or segments of your employees, what isn't working and why something didn't work.

If something that isn't working comes about because of decisions, *you need to own the decisions.* Admit to your employees that what is not working is because of a decision *mistake* you made. Acknowledge your mistakes to your employees without trying to spin the results of your mistakes to them. Don't let your ego stand in the way of being honest about what's not working. Instead of avoiding responsibility, identify what caused the failures and what needs to be done to fix the problem.

Making this approach means you have to allow yourself a degree of vulnerability. That runs counter to the desire many business owners have to appear all-knowing. But it will help you to build leadership credibility with your employees

Ask your employees to help you by providing ideas of what could be done to correct a problem, do something better, or take advantage of an opportunity.

Once you have determined the new path, you must get your employees on board. Getting support for changes is more likely to happen if your employees hear from you why the thing that is being changed is not working.

How you communicate what needs to be done will significantly affect whether you can get your employees on board. Your communication announcing the changes should reflect confidence in the benefit of doing what you want. If the communication goes well, employees will radiate an unshakable belief that what needs to be done differently is the best option.

Business owners who are good leaders do not allow unsuccessful approaches to continue. When changes are needed, they make the required changes happen. How you handle bringing about a shift in company plans or procedures will reflect your leadership ability.

KEY POINT: Your employees will be more likely to embrace the changes you want if your company culture embraces a willingness to adapt and adopt.

Common Trait #3: Curious by Nature

Curiosity may have killed the cat, but it has benefitted every successful business owner I've ever met. Curiosity leads you to ask questions, explore options, and challenge conventions. And all those actions can lead to breakthrough ideas, cost savings, improved client service, and problems prevented. Think of curiosity as the first cousin to innovation and the precursor to inspiration.

Some businesses require a curious owner. Suppose you are not curious by nature, and the business you like needs it. In that case, you should either consider different companies to start that don't require curiosity as a necessity or consider hiring or engaging someone curious by nature to be part of your team.

Common Trait #4: People Oriented

When I asked the SBFs to rate their people skills, most, but not all, claimed to have good people skills. However, some of the SBFs shared their belief that they not only do not have what is often called good people skills but rather have poor people skills.

Not surprisingly, one SBF acknowledged to a group of business owners, including me, that he is an introvert who naturally does not enjoy interacting with others. He said, "I don't even like most people." The group had a collective chuckle.

He added, however, that he was confident his employees viewed him as a good leader even though he didn't have excellent people skills. He said he thought his employees viewed him as an enthusiastic winner who was good at motivating them. He shared that one of the reasons for this view was that he accepted responsibility for decisions when they didn't work.

Although the people skills of a business owner help make a business succeed, they are not essential. So, yes, you can be a successful business owner even if you aren't people-oriented by using your other abilities.

Common Trait #5: Mental Ability

Among the most common traits shared by most SBFs is that they have been blessed with more intelligence/common sense than the average person. They have the mental ability to think through challenges and come up with solutions that sometimes make the difference between failure, success, and great success. They are problem solvers, and business owners need that skill in abundance.

Common Trait #6: Confidence

SBFs typically see themselves as "take-charge" people who exude confidence. Being a take-charge person helps their employees to share in their faith for the future of the business. When owners of businesses demonstrate confidence, they leave no doubt in the minds of their employees about what needs to be done for the company. They assume responsibility for their companies and accept that there is no one above them to take the blame.

If you're starting a business, you need to be confident that you have what it takes to get good results for the company to happen. Is it any surprise that nearly every SBF said that they have self-confidence? That trait is essential when things are not working out as quickly or as well as you would like.

SBFs have confidence in their ability to take calculated risks. Although your success or failure with your start-up business is mostly in your own hands, some things will not be within your control to overcome. What happened to many companies during the Pandemic is an example of this.

Many SBFs built up their confidence because they had experienced success while working for others. They have learned from experience that they can trust themselves to get things. They enjoy making decisions and accept responsibility for them. They can acknowledge they were wrong when they were wrong. They can sleep at night without being traumatized by the fear of failing.

Naturally, others see them as having confidence when they see their business founders make bold moves while displaying an optimistic view of the chances of successful actions. SBFs are not afraid of failing. When things don't go as planned, they are persistent. They will think about how to shift gears and be confident they can make things work.

In contrast, glass-half-empty people are prone to giving up when things don't go as planned. Consequently, it's difficult for a pessimist to appear to employees as confident

The SBFs not only had confidence in themselves but also in the value delivered by their products and/or services. Good luck conveying confidence to your prospects if you don't believe in the value of your products and services.

Common Trait #7: Ability to Effectively Wear Many Hats

There's a reason the expression is a cliché: It's true. The average day in a business owner's life may feel like they are going from one type of business activity to another. They may be working on sales issues, attending a marketing meeting, and then one on operations — with minor crisis interruptions.

The ultimate responsibility for wearing many different hats lies with the business owner. For someone who gets bored quickly, this lifestyle is a perfect fit. Others may find wearing many hats to be stressful.

Common Trait #8: Obsessive About Making the Business Succeed

Obsession is often considered a negative quality. However, many successful business owners recognize it in themselves and harness it. While the SBFs generally did not call themselves obsessive, they did acknowledge that they are driven to succeed.

That driving force often pushes them to think about making their businesses successful, even when not at work, which is a familiar feeling among most SBFs. Several mentioned how they had to fight against becoming too obsessive with their businesses, often pushing themselves hard to achieve their business objectives.

After one member mentioned thinking about business and making notes on things related to the business at night, they all admitted they did that. To them, business problems were challenges and opportunities requiring them to respond versus remaining passive.

I asked the SBFs how they would rate themselves on a scale of one to ten on the desire to succeed. All rated themselves with an intensity scale of eight, nine, or ten.

Some of them confessed that their companies, for better or worse, had become the primary purpose in their life, particularly during the early years. One shared that her obsession with her start-up business was the cause of her divorce from a man she loved.

Common Trait #9: Comfortable Being the Final Decision Maker

Business owners are the final decision-makers in their businesses. So, perhaps the distinction is this: Most SBFs *enjoy responsibility*. It shouldn't surprise you that when I asked how they felt about making the final decisions in their businesses, all the SBFs responded that they liked it.

Ultimately, your start-up company's results will depend on you — your plans, actions, policies, and practices. You can't blame "the boss" anymore because that's you! And you know the buck will stop with you if you are the business owner.

Unafraid of mistakes, SBFs make decisions that sometimes involve bold moves. And they sleep a night without being traumatized by the fear of failure. They generally accept responsibility for their own choices, even if some find it hard to admit when they were wrong.

Honestly, the average business owner makes dozens of decisions, big and small, every day. As a business owner, you may have to decide, in the same week, whether or not to:

- Hire or fire an employee
- Shut down a product or service line
- Raise prices on a product or service
- Launch a marketing campaign

- Expand the company's office space

- Approve or disapprove a budget

Close your eyes and visualize potential interactions where you have the final say on things like the above examples. How did you imagine yourself in these situations? You're on the right path if you feel excited, even invigorating.

Unless you're comfortable being the final decision-maker, think twice before diving into starting a business, and think hard and long about becoming a business owner. If your palms got a little sweaty out of dread of making the decisions, owning a company may be very stressful.

Common Trait #10 Willing to Assume Risk

SBFs can calculate and take risks without having them affect their ability to perform. They have the temperament to perform well while having the pressure of calculated risks hanging over their heads. Without this trait, starting a business could result in the founder experiencing too much stress to function.

Business owners assume different types of risks. Uncertainty is just part of being the owner of a business.

One type of risk is that your business decisions will not work. Surprise, surprise — some of your choices will fail.

SBFs accept that some of the things they thought would work won't.

Another type of risk is the financial risk of starting a business. Start-ups are calculated risks. The reality is that privately-owned business start-ups have high failure rates. Because of this, you need to identify the financial risk that makes you comfortable. Concerning the financial risk of a start-up business failing, a willingness to assume the risk of company failure is a trait of most SBFs. They embrace a disciplined, risk-taking view toward starting their businesses.

Even when you've done everything possible to eliminate the risks, there may be factors outside your control. So, there is the risk of the unknown jeopardizing your success. For example, many start-up businesses had good beginnings and then went out of business because of the Pandemic.

In assessing themselves, SBFs say they are comfortable taking necessary business risks. They have a mindset that allows them to operate effectively while taking calculated chances from the reality that new businesses have inherent threats. Taking the "big leap" often required many SBFs to chuck the safety net of working for someone else. Most were required to put all their assets at risk with a personal guarantee of company loans or lines of credit. In addition to the personal guarantees, most were required to give liens against their home equity to secure the loans needed for their businesses.

Accepting the risk of a start-up business failing is not for everyone. The Director of Acquisitions for a large company mentioned that he would love to start a mergers and acquisition company but would probably never do it. When I asked why he hadn't, the answer was he would not be able to sleep at night if he knew that his income depended on closing a deal that might or might not happen.

Common Trait #11: Focused

I can summarize in one word the skill necessary to see beyond and work through the frustrations and aggravation you're bound to encounter when your business is young. It is "Focus." SBFs can typically focus intently on their objectives and stay focused until they solve the challenges. Sometimes the cost of this focus is pushing other things to the side so that you can focus on what needs to be done to get what you want from your new business.

Successful SBFs address specific business objectives without being diverted to tangential business activities. Typically, they can zero in on achieving vital goals, an essential skill.

Most SBFs said they are highly focused and good at prioritizing what merits their attention. Many had systems to help them pinpoint what needed to get done on any day,

35

week, or month. Then, they accomplished the essential things that made a difference.

One SBF told me that she felt her competitive advantage and secret to success was her ability to focus. She said she had the discipline to remain focused on "big picture matters" even when it sometimes meant delaying handling day-to-day problems that could easily have absorbed her time.

Common Trait #12: Persistence

To get a start-up through its early years, persistence is essential. Most SBFs said that the first years were more challenging than predicted. In fact, according to Skynova, the small business resource, 36% of the 250 entrepreneurs surveyed said they considered quitting before their businesses took off.

Most of the SBFs responded that their perseverance helped them overcome obstacles they encountered during the early stages of their businesses. Many of them faced what seemed to be impossible situations but were persistent in finding a way to solve them. They expressed how their persistence helped their companies to survive.

Business founders need to find a way to overcome hurdles, no matter what happens. They will go after solutions with tenacity until they overcome the inevitable obstacles confronting start-ups. They don't blame bad luck when things are failing. Instead, they look for the problems behind the failures and overcome them.

Most of the SBFs viewed their self-discipline at work as essential to their perseverance.

Choosing a goal and sticking to it changes everything.- Scott Reed

Success is not final; failure is not fatal: it is the courage to continue that counts.- Winston Churchill

Common Trait #13: Able to Handle Stress

For most business owners, stress is like a shadow, an annoying younger sibling who follows you wherever you go. You can't rid yourself of it, so you have to learn how to deal with it. You need to manage it without believing you can eliminate it because you can't.

Interestingly, when asked if they could handle stress, particularly during the early years of their start-ups, most felt that they didn't let the stress sap them. They could function well with what they had to do despite the pressure.

Sources of stress vary by the individual and business type, but when you start a business, a common cause is encountering unexpected challenges. Most of your business days will bring some measure of it, often from things they had not anticipated. But if you don't control your stress, it will not only hurt your work and demotivate your employees.

Common Trait #14: Strategic Thinker

Stepping back periodically to think strategically about the big picture is one of the most important things you can do. Most of the SBFs responded that they viewed themselves as strategic thinkers but often spent less time than they wanted thinking strategically about their businesses because they had to spend time "putting out fires" when managing the day-to-day operations.

It is recommended that you schedule time each week to stop to look at and challenge whether your company's goals and strategies will lead to attaining your long-term vision for your company. Evaluate whether you are handling things in ways that will lead you to reach your company's long-term objective. Try to see your business with fresh eyes when doing this.

SBFs set measurable, transparent strategic goals. They track the progress needed to achieve their objectives when their businesses started and later as they grew.

Common Trait #15: Ambitious

It is not surprising that SBFs are typically ambitious. That's why they start businesses. An old business adage calls ambition "the ingredient that makes dough rise." Without a robust and ambitious nature, a start-up will unlikely go very far.

Common Trait #16: Willingness to Sacrifice

Delayed gratification is a common theme among SBFs. Did they put off today's rewards for a more significant return tomorrow? They postponed the payoff in the short term for the big payback in the long term. Sacrificing took place both financially and with lifestyle.

Most SBFs sacrificed financially in the early years of their businesses to achieve their longer-term financial dreams. It was necessary for most of them because it typically takes a while for new companies to become financially profitable. According to Skynova, a small business resource, the average time for a business to become economically beneficial is three years, based on their survey of 250 entrepreneurs.

No matter how successful their businesses initially were, most just pulled out enough money to get by. Why? So that they can keep the money in their business to help it grow. Sacrificing and living a modest lifestyle in the early years helps finance the bigger payoff down the road.

Another area of sacrifice was giving up personal and family time. Most of the SBFs admitted they had to work on creating separate times for their personal lives. They felt they were not good about preventing their businesses from becoming an all-consuming detriment to their lives outside work.

For this reason, your family needs to understand that you will have tremendous demands on you in the early years of your business. As a result, this isn't for everyone. One woman told me she wanted to leave her job to open a retail store, so I discussed the sacrifices necessary to start a new business. After we talked, she agreed that she did not want to make the sacrifices needed to start a business at her stage of life.

Common Trait #17: Troubles with Time Management

One of the questions I asked was whether the SBFs felt competent at managing their time. The answer: Not so much.

Time management was one of the areas where most shared a weakness. It was common to hear how time management was one of the biggest challenges, particularly during their business operation's first year. Few had mastered using their time without letting the business consume them.

You want to manage your time to deliver the most significant benefit to your business *and* your family. You will make much more effective use of your days by delegating or outsourcing low-impact tasks that are high-time-drain activities.

One SBF, who had an accounting degree, said he spent 20% or more of his time doing the books for his company during his first several months in business. He said one of the best things he did was turn over the bookkeeping responsibility to a part-time, outside bookkeeper. That freed up time for what he should have done as the business owner.

Common Trait #18: Live Within Means

There is one character trait that you might find interesting. The SBIFs said that they lived within their means. And what happens when you live within your means? You have less pressure to take money from the business and have more to reinvest.

The homes they lived in are an example of this. When I asked SBFs whether their home cost less than they could afford or if they were stretching to meet a mortgage, they responded that the value was significantly less than they could afford. *Not one SBF said they owned homes they could not afford.*

Common Trait #19: Self Accountable

In short, SBFs hold themselves responsible for the goals, actions, and results, whatever the outcomes. As a business owner, you will need to do the same. The person you will have to inspire most to get things done *is you*. There will be no one to push you but yourself.

Your business will depend on you to recognize what's needed. And then to make sure it gets done! There will be no one to make sure you follow through with things. So you need to be *self-accountable* for whatever happens in your business. Getting the results you want for your start-up business will occur only if you identify the things holding back the results from happening and then find ways to neutralize or eliminate these things.

Common Trait #20: Do not Befriend Their Employees

One of the traits that most SBFs have is that they do not befriend their employees. Imagine how decisions become more manageable when owners don't have to decide between what's right with the company and their friendship with an individual employee.

How can you discipline a friend? It's difficult. When I first became a co-owner of Tipton, I made the mistake of having a close friendship with one of the executives. At that time, I believed that he and I were good friends, and we spent time with our spouses. It didn't take me long to learn that this can cause problems for some employees to feel that I was giving special treatment to the executive. The reality is that I was giving him special treatment. I allowed him to take advantage of the friendship, which upset some other employees.

Common Trait #21: Accept the Need for Them to Handle Confrontations

Owning a business requires you to engage in confrontations. It's a fact of life. It does not mean you like confrontations. It's Okay that many SBFs, myself included, find conflict unpleasant. However, you cannot run a business without occasionally handling disputes with your employees, vendors, customers, or clients.

It would help if you recognized the need to handle conflicts and decide how you will manage conflicts when they arise.

Common Trait #22: Keep Emotions in Check

When a business owner gets emotional and yells out a comment in the heat of the moment, it has more impact than when another employee does. As a result, most successful SBFs have learned to reign in their emotions after becoming owners.

Statements made out of anger or frustration can be highly destructive. When you publicly berate an employee over an error, you lower the morale of ALL the employees who witness it. What's more, comments made in anger by business owners cause irreparable damage to the relationship with the person who's the object of your anger.

Common Trait #23: Analyze Before Acting

Start-ups inevitably have problems. If the situation allows it, analyze it before making decisions. Before you try to solve a problem, identify the source. Don't jump into action too soon. Take the time to investigate marketing needs, customer profiles, and budgets before taking the plunge.

Conclusion

Do you share most of these character traits that are common with SBFs? If not, identify how you'll overcome these gaps in your trait makeup before starting a business.

PART TWO: LEARNING FROM SBF MISTAKES

Perhaps as important as knowing what SBFs did right to make their start-up businesses successful, I will, in Part Two, *share the mistakes they made* with their earlier start-up businesses that were responsible for the failure of their earlier enterprises. I will also share the mistakes made by SBFs with their current companies that they had to overcome on the way to success.

In Chapter Three, we will look at the type of mistakes that several of the SBFs said hurt their businesses, and in Chapter Four, we will look at the kind of mistakes that one or a few of the SBFs said hurt their businesses.

Learning about what they did wrong will help you avoid making the same mistakes.

CHAPTER THREE-MISTAKES MADE BY SEVERAL SBFs

Introduction

Many entrepreneurs now running successful companies had owned previous businesses that failed. A study by Skynova said that about one in four entrepreneurs failed at least once with previous businesses before succeeding with their current companies.

Sometimes, failure happens because of something that the business founders of their start-ups could not have foreseen. An obvious example is the Pandemic, which caused many businesses to fail.

But in other cases, there may have been a better outcome if things could have been done differently. One of the most frequent comments I've heard from SBFs who had experienced previous start-up failures is that they've grown from their failures. The knowledge they gained helped them achieve their current business successes.

Davie Fogarty, the entrepreneur who created Adelaide, which generates hundreds of millions in sales, had <u>six failed businesses</u>. Mr. Fogarty told *The Daily Mail* that his six business failures "pushed me to this journey of learning new skills, of learning digital marketing and giving me the tools for better businesses."

Another example is Travis Kalanick, the co-founder of Uber. After launching tech start-up Scour, he had to file for bankruptcy. But he didn't let that stop him from achieving great success with Uber.

Many SBFs said that the successes of their current businesses resulted partly from what they had learned by making mistakes previously. They shared different mistakes they had made either with previous companies they started or with their current companies that significantly hurt their businesses. Following are mistakes you need to learn from and avoid making with your start-up businesses.

1. Underfinanced businesses
2. No or insufficient demand for their products or services
3. Didn't target the right customer or clients
4. Businesses started were wrong fits for founders
5. Didn't have a business plan or financial projections
6. Didn't control the cash going out
7. Poor human resource approach
8. Not having a clear long-term company vision
9. Hired too many relatives and friends
10. Underestimated competition
11. Didn't need experience
12. Opened business before the business was ready
13. Giving risky credit
14. Being too optimistic

15. Didn't spend enough time and money on the website

16. Not having needed technology

17. Poor turn of inventory

18. Customers didn't comply with agreed-upon payment terms

19. Took too many risks

20. Too slow to make needed changes

Let's look at the mistakes that several SBFs said hurt their businesses and consider how this information will help you avoid your mistakes when you start your business.

Mistake To Avoid #1: Underfinanced Businesses

The most common reason mentioned by SBFs for the failures of their earlier businesses was that their earlier start-up businesses didn't have adequate funding to survive until the business thrived. These SBFs felt their companies could have become great success stories with adequate financing. Instead, they failed and closed up.

Don't under-capitalize your start-up. A new business needs sufficient funding to sustain itself before it begins generating positive cash flow.

You would never take a road trip without enough gas in your car. Why jeopardize your new business by denying it resources before it has a chance to succeed? Give your start-up business adequate financing to increase the likelihood of it succeeding.

Pro-tip: The funding required for start-up businesses to survive typically *exceeds what you thought optimistically would be needed.* This is because there are so many unknowns in the early years. So be conservative about how much you'll need to operate and start with more significant funding based on everything going the way you wish.

Because so many start-ups that fail do so because of inadequate funding, they spend the needed time to get the right amount of financing from suitable sources. You must focus on your company's financing even if you find doing so to be an unpleasant activity for you to do. Financing your business is so important that I devote an entire chapter to funding your start-up later in this book.

Mistake To Avoid #2: No or Insufficient Demand for Their Products or Services

Some failed start-ups didn't succeed because their founders looked before they leaped. It is prevalent for those starting businesses to be too impulsive. They want to get things going quickly, but this can be a mistake. Unfortunately, they were wrong in their belief that prospects existed who wanted the products or services their start-up businesses offered at the prices they charged for the products or services.

Before opening their businesses, most small and midsize business founders did not do even minimal interviews with potential customers or clients. In many cases, the products or services offered by their start-ups would have looked different, or they would not have moved ahead in starting the companies if they had conducted fundamental research about the potential demand for the products or services.

In other words, the time to find out if there is a product-market fit *is before you start the business*. Instead, they skipped this step in their eagerness to open their doors.

Pro-tip: Before you start a business from scratch, be sure that demand for the product or service you intend to sell is there — and that you can sell it at a profitable price. If market demand for a product or service does not already exist, you may be courting failure.

Your research should involve interviewing a few potential customers or clients to learn if they value what your start-up would be selling and how much they would pay.

One SBF's description of why her precious start-up failed should warn all would-be entrepreneurs: "The customers for my product don't know they needed it, and I could not make them aware of it." Few start-up businesses succeed in these types of situations.

One SBF's previous business start-up was a concept he simultaneously opened in several retail stores. The founder was so sure there would be a demand for his service that he did not research to determine its level of need. The need wasn't there, and, as a result, it closed up within one year of starting the business. With some relatively inexpensive market research, that business failure could have been avoided.

NOTE: This issue about demand should not be as big a concern for you if you buy a franchise to start your business because you can validate with current franchisees as to the need for the product or service based on their experience selling it.

Mistake To Avoid #3: Didn't Target the Right Customers or Clients

Your chances of business being a success are much greater if you know who the prospects most likely are to be your customers or clients. No matter how well you do many other things for your start-up, it won't matter if you don't target the best prospects for your offering. If you go after the wrong customers, your company will likely fail even if your products and services are excellent.

So, do what you can afford to do to verify that who you think are your potential customers or clients are good prospects for what you will be offering. Once you know your targeted prospects, you should try to learn their key factors. After you know this, you should create the marketing strategies and messages likely to attract prospects.

Also, after receiving this type of information about your prospects, you may discover you have to change the products or services your business will offer to make them more attractive to their customer or client prospects. Changes might involve such things as including additional features or service warranties.

If you don't get this information, you may use the wrong marketing strategy to launch your business. Many SBFs said their earlier start-up businesses failed because they used the wrong approach to market their products or services correctly. The companies might have succeeded had their marketing been better. Targeting the wrong customer or client or appealing to them in the wrong way is a common mistake made by start-up businesses.

So, if your product is intended primarily for 12- to 25-year-olds, aim the marketing money at media that target them alone. A music video station geared toward young adults might work.

If you are trying to get the word out about your new business to adult men, consider using a sports station in your local area, as sports coverage has a high percentage of adult males.

Another mistake is not identifying their prospective customers and where customers or clients are located. Many have wasted large portions of their marketing budgets by targeting prospects living in areas that made it unlikely that they would buy from the start-up businesses. The marketing money could have been used more effectively.

If your business focuses primarily on a limited geographic area within an area, don't diffuse your kickoff budget on media that reaches beyond that area.

It is essential that you know the geographic area where your prospects live. To spend marketing money trying to attract those living further away won't give you a good return on your advertising money spent. For example, one start-up bakery spent its launch opening marketing dollars on radio ads blanketing a whole city; 95% of that population lived at least a 15-minute drive away from the bakery. The results showed very few sales occurred with those living beyond 15 minutes from the store. The owner should have focused his launch marketing on targeting those who live within 15 minutes of the bakery. The bakery went out of business within one year of opening.

Suppose you intend to do a survey, even a very inexpensive survey, to help you determine who your prospects are and critical things about them. In that case, it is essential that the right questions for the survey be used and that the questions are posed to the right participants who meet specific demographics.

Many start-up businesses conduct such surveys without outside help. However, you should engage a professional to do the survey if you have a sufficient budget. Knowing your prospects and critical factors, such as their location, will help you develop the best strategy and messaging to drive potential buyers to your website or store. It might even assist in creating appealing product packaging that can significantly help your sales.

Mistake To Avoid #4: Businesses Started Were Wrong Fits for Founders

One of the primary causes of start-up business failure, not surprisingly, is selecting *the wrong business to start.* Bad fits gave certain founders fits and made it easier to give up on the companies before they had exhausted their chances of success!

Some start-up businesses were terrible fits for their founders because the businesses didn't match the long-term visions the founders wanted for their futures. Before they selected the company to start up, the founders should have taken the time to write a clear vision statement, in 100 words or less, of what they wanted their lives to be five to 10 years in the future.

The following are other reasons start-up businesses turned out to be bad fits:

- Their founders did not have a passion for the products or services offered by the businesses
- Their founders lacked needed expertise or experience to run the businesses

- Their founders didn't have the personal or behavioral traits required to lead the company

Even if you are uncomfortable wearing many hats as the owner, you will probably have to during the first years of your business. The ones you want to take off are those that require you to work in your areas of weakness or are uncomfortable doing because they don't fit who they are.

Some SBFs failed in their earlier businesses because they were required to do too much in the way of activities that needed them to have good skills that they didn't have. Or activities that required experience they didn't have.

For example, some businesses require business owners to interact well with employees, customers/ clients, and suppliers. Yet many business founders fail at things that extroverts enjoy, such as interacting with employees, customers/clients, or suppliers.

So, print this on your coffee mug: *Your talent alone will not guarantee the success of your business.* To launch a profitable company that achieves your vision of success, you need to use your talents well and not take on a business where you would be required to do things that don't fit you.

Later in this book, I devote a chapter to help you pick the right business for you and how to get a good fit between the founder of a start-up business and the company.

Mistake To Avoid #5: Didn't Have a Business Plan or Financial Projections

Some SBFs made the mistake of not creating a business plan and financial projections before starting the businesses and regretted it. It resulted in many bad decisions in their previous start-ups that would not have happened had the founders reviewed financial projections.

Although it would be beneficial for all founders to have business plans before their businesses start operating, many SBFs started acknowledging that they did not have them created. As a result, their businesses sometimes moved along in a rudderless manner.

For example, some SBFs focused on growth rather than profits. They launched with low prices to bring about sales. They burned through their initial capital too quickly by pricing too low and didn't have the money to continue operating.

For them, focusing on growing faster by offering low prices was a formula for disaster. With the guidance of financial projections, they would have realized that they should have focused more on profitable growth rather than growing as fast as possible through low prices.

They realized too late that they should have focused more on profitable expansion. The businesses burned through their initial capital and didn't have the money to continue. After all, showing growth in sales on your financial statement won't help you pay the bills without cash to pay the bills.

A "lowest-prices" strategy can be a race to the bottom, creating sales volume that can cause the business to fail! So, if your salespeople might want you to say yes to low-ball orders, as the owner, you need to be able to say no to deals that won't make money.

The SBFs thought they were Okay with the low pricing they were charging because they did not have break-even projections. If they had made such projections, they would have realized their businesses could not survive on their charging prices.

So, before starting your business, get a break-even analysis projection that considers all your costs. When break-even projections are correctly made, they consider all the operating costs. For example, considering employee costs would include *all* the additional expenses tied to their employment, such as employee benefits, space, equipment, training, etc.

The break-even analysis projection points out the sales volume and gross profit needed to be generated to eliminate losses for your new business. It is then easy to estimate the required net sales volume you need to reach to avoid losing money.

When you do a break-even analysis, you may realize that you wouldn't turn a profit unless you sell your products or services for higher prices. As a result, you may have to increase prices to attain a needed minimum gross profit (sales price less the cost of the merchandise or purchase cost of goods).

This break-even analysis includes fixed costs, which are those that do not change with increases or decreases in sales volumes. It also includes your variable costs, which directly track increases or decreases in sales volumes. If there are no sales, there are no variable costs.

After seeing the break-even analysis projection, you may need to make management decisions regarding controlling expenses. It is a typical result of creating the analysis.

After your break-even analysis projection, you can create a budget for what you can spend before your business opens and during the first year of its operation. You can use it to monitor how things are going by monitoring results versus your budget. The monitoring results may indicate that you need to make needed adjustments.

Of course, the quality of the projection is important. For example, use conservative, realistic sales forecasts rather than highly optimistic ones—the more accurate the sales forecast, the lower the risk of spending too much.

Many founders were too optimistic about projecting expenses. They also, in many cases, significantly misjudged or ignored the actual cost of operating the business relating to such things as:

- Utilities
- Equipment payments
- Different types of insurance they would have to get
- Charges for using specific sales channels, such as websites that charge for each transaction
- Licenses and permits are required by various governments
- The fringe cost of employees beyond the employees' salaries

I could go on and on. The point? You can't possibly know what you need to charge if you don't know your expenses in advance.

Mistake To Avoid #6: Didn't Control the Cash Going Out

Some SBFs felt that the start-up businesses they previously started were doomed because they allowed them to begin with too much overhead for the generated sales volume. Their optimism about generating a larger amount of sales for their businesses led them to incur costs that were out of line with sales results.

The businesses often committed to fixed costs that they could not easily reduce. For example, one SBF mentioned that he bought a large warehouse for his start-up to use because he was confident the space would be needed to handle the sales volume he was confident would take place. However, sales were much less than expected, and the warehouse was half-empty most of the time. As a result, the warehouse cost drained the company's cash resources.

There are several ways to keep expenses in line with revenue during your early years of operation, which might apply to your situation. One way is to ask the party leasing you space for help during your early years of operations by allowing you to pay your rent based on a percentage of your sales rather than a fixed amount. Many landlords have helped start-up tenants this way during the early period of their operations.

Public warehousing is an underutilized alternative that can be very helpful, particularly for start-up and early-stage companies. You only pay for what you need with public warehousing, which is particularly important for a start-up business because no one can determine what sales activity they will generate. Public warehouses allow companies to set up temporary warehouse and distribution arrangements during the first years of operation when they are unsure of their needs. Public warehouses usually have full-time workers all year round, thus avoiding much of the inefficiency of your start-up having to hire workers not fully used.

Another way to control your overhead applies if you are starting a retail or distribution business is by asking your suppliers to put a certain amount of their inventory in your store on consignment so you won't have money tied up in this inventory. You won't pay for the consigned merchandise items until the items are sold.

Mistake To Avoid #7: Poor Human Resource Approach

Several SBFs expressed that their previous start-up and current companies had suffered from poor hiring practices. These practices negatively impacted their businesses in significant ways.

Several start-up business owners made the mistake of trying to do too much. They had spread themselves too thin. They felt they should have hired one or more management-level employees to help them. Without any other managers in the new business, he found that he was spending all his time on day-to-day things and managing different parts of the company for which he had no experience.

Because of this, he didn't have the time available to focus on big-picture things that could have made a big difference in the business results. He believed his company would have succeeded if he had employed one or two capable managers to help him manage the business.

Another human resource-related thing they did poorly involved their poor hiring methods. They had too many new employees who turned out to be duds instead of diamonds and didn't work out. As a result, he wasted time and money replacing the employees and wasted onboarding replacement employees.

When businesses are in the start-up and initial early period of operations, there are significant unknowns about work needs. So during this period of operations, you should be thinking of "lean staffing" until your business becomes established enough that you can predict staffing needs.

When you follow the lead staffing approach, you hire only enough full-time employees to do the job for a regular workload. So, you don't have the cost of full-time employees when you don't need them. You fill in when you need more help. When your workload exceeds the regular workload during rush periods or, for whatever reason, things are busy, you handle it by engaging part-time workers or workers from temporary employee service. The idea is to pay only for the hours these people do work. Depending on the country where you operate, you may not have to pay part-time, and temp workers benefits such as sick pay, vacation pay, holidays, and health insurance.

Another area that SBFs wish they had done differently was to hire full-time employees for certain services instead of engaging independent contractors. For example, they could have engaged outside commissioned sales representatives who get paid based on sales results rather than hiring salespeople.

Engaging independent contractors makes it easier to control expenses because you pay them only as you need the services.

Note: Laws differ in countries regarding factors determining whether a person is an independent contractor versus an employee. So, find out what applies where you live.

Another common thing that SBFs did wrong in hiring was hiring employees without checking out their references and doing credit and criminal background checks. It saved the money of checking out the employee prospects before hiring them as employees but cost them much more due to them being bad employees.

Who does this? Who hires employees without checking their references and doing credit and criminal background checks? Sadly, many of our SBFs admitted that they had done it in the past and hurt their start-up businesses.

One SBF said he would not have hired his first three employees if he had done his homework. He added that his poor job of engaging the three employees cost his company money.

So, why didn't they check out the new employee candidates before hiring them? There were two reasons given. One was they were in a rush to do the hiring, and the other was that it costs little money to check the prospects.

I should mention that the wrong kind of employee could become a danger to you and your other employees. It's worth getting criminal background checks

Several SBFs said they had made a mistake by hiring employees who didn't share the values they expected from their employees. After experiencing problems with hiring employees with values they did not like, they started to address what they expected in values with prospective employees before hiring them. They then hired only employees they believed shared the core values they wanted for their business.

If core values are shared among your employees, they will be more likely to feel like they are part of a community they believe in. This belief will help create a good culture that will result in greater and higher quality output. This culture will increase employee retention, saving time and money in hiring replacements and onboarding them.

It's a lot easier to identify and judge the intelligence and experience of your new hire prospects than it is, but you must try to hire those who share your core values. So during your interview with these prospects, discuss the core values you are looking for with your employees. Ask them to share their views on whether the core values are good fits for them.

When you hire employees who don't share the same core values, it's almost inevitable that there will be morale problems with other employees. There is also a greater likelihood of tension and even hostility.

Mistake to Avoid #8: Not Having a Clear Long-Term Company Vision

Some of the founders of businesses that failed had in common that they did not have a clear vision for the company's long-term future. As a result, employee decisions and actions were often without needed direction.

A written company vision statement guides employees to follow a series of flawed shifting goals that do not lead to the desired vision. A vision statement shared with the employees would have helped everyone stay on course and work towards a shared vision for the company. They didn't develop a clear vision for employees to follow.

Before hiring any employees for your start-up business, create your vision for your new company and share it with prospective employees. You don't want to develop strategic plans for your start-up business without knowing they will lead to achieving the long-term company vision you want to achieve. After you see the company vision you want to reach, you develop the goals, strategies, and action plans to achieve the vision.

Many start-up businesses have exhausted their financial resources before they become profitable because they didn't have a clear vision of where the company energies should be directed. Too much time was wasted by several SBFs and their employees doing tasks that didn't support or lead to attaining the company vision.

Every product or service your company provides should directly relate to achieving your company's vision. Your goals and strategic plans should be the roadmap to success. This roadmap makes it easy to make corrections when anything diverts from the road you need to take.

Before you open the doors to your new business, be sure you have clear goals and strategies that align with your company's vision. If all company decisions are consistent with these goals, everyone in your company will be focused on achieving the company vision.

It's up to you as the leader of your business to keep the company vision in front of your employees so they don't lose sight of it when doing their day-to-day activities.

Conclusion

The eight mistakes shared in this chapter were common for those who started businesses. Think twice before you do the things that helped destroy the start-up businesses founded by these SBFs.

CHAPTER FOUR-MISTAKES MADE BY ONE OR A FEW SBFs

You can learn from some mistakes made by one or only a few of the SBFs. These, like those mistakes shared in Chapter Three, are mistakes that you should not repeat.

Mistake To Avoid #9: Hired Too Many Relatives and Friends

One day at lunch, an SBF told me about a previous business he had started that had failed. I asked him why the company failed, and his answer was different than any I had heard from other SBFs who I had asked the same question.

He told me that the business failed because he had started the business mostly with employees who were relatives or friends of his. The SBF had wanted to surround himself with employees who were friends and relatives because he thought they would give an extra effort beyond what others might provide.

But it didn't work out that way. Some of them were unqualified for what he needed. Their attitude and feeling that they should be treated special caused problems at work. He added that it also hurt and, in some cases, destroyed his relationships with friends and relatives outside of work.

He told me that he learned an expensive lesson and, as a result, did not hire any relatives or friends for his next business start-up, which became successful.

Mistake To Avoid #10: Underestimated Competition

A few SBFs said their previous start-up businesses had failed because they underestimated the established competition and found it challenging to take business away from them. These SBFs misread the tea leaves and didn't have an effective strategy to deal with the competition.

They had no Plan B to deal with competition. It was particularly true when competing against larger established companies that bought their materials for less, had more robust brand recognition, or had loyal customers or clients.

Mistake to Avoid #11: Didn't Have Needed Experience

A few SBFs expressed their belief that their previous businesses failed because they were not adequately prepared to own and lead a business when they started their previous companies. They felt they didn't have the experience to address the obstacles and challenges they faced when the previous start-up businesses opened.

Mistake to Avoid #12: Opened Business Before the Business Was Ready

Optimism has a funny way of distorting reality. One result is that SBFs often underestimate how long it would take to get their earlier businesses ready to start. They opened their businesses before they should have done so. For example, they opened before their employees were adequately trained.

A friend of mine opened a restaurant with great recipes and locations. So far, so good. Sadly, he did not allow adequate time to train his personnel. The food was disappointing; the service was terrible. The restaurant closed within its first year of operation.

It's not necessary to reinvent the wheel. However, it is necessary to do whatever it takes to make the wheel roll more efficiently. A start-up mustn't be open for business until the employees can provide predictable, good to superb execution of everything that needs to be done in your business. It should be one of the critical philosophies of anyone starting a new business.

So, be conservative in predicting how long it will take to get your business up and running. Consider the time it will take to hire and train your initial employees, the time to get the premises ready, and the inventory in stock. Then, if possible, do a limited type of opening to identify problems and solve them before a grand opening.

Mistake to Avoid #13: Giving Risky Credit

One SBF had previously started an import business that failed because a company he sold a lot of merchandise to on credit could not pay for it when the money came due. He gave too high a credit line to the customer, a retail store chain, with questionable credit. The "red flags" were there in the credit report, but he gave a high credit line because he wanted to take the sales order for a significant amount of merchandise.

His business went into a cash flow bind shortly after the customer didn't pay for the merchandise when the payment was due. After collection agencies and attorneys got involved in retrieving the money owed him, he got some of it. But it was too late for his business when he received it.

Mistake to Avoid #14: Being Too Optimistic

Some have made the mistake of starting too big. It's exciting to have a business idea that you "know will work." But don't allow yourself to be too optimistic. Take it slowly by first testing and then tweaking your business model to have an improved model before you do a big "rollout."

Several years earlier, one SBF started a business with a service he was sure would succeed. Within one year, the company failed.

Why did it fail? He was so optimistic about the sales that would take place that instead of starting with one location, he opened eight locations at about the same time! Had he tested the business model in one location first, he would have seen the challenges and made adjustments before expanding. By starting the business with eight locations, his company ran out of money before it had a chance to correct its problems.

Mistake to Avoid #15: Didn't Spend Enough Time and Money on the Website

A few SBFs who had previously started businesses that failed before they started their current successful companies said their biggest mistake was not having a great professional-looking website before they opened. They had made the mistake of deciding not to spend much time or money creating a professional-looking website.

Many of your prospective customers or clients will make an initial judgment about your start-up business based on the quality of your website. So invest the time to make your website's design, navigation, and copy as compelling as possible.

Many outstanding independent contractors will bid on the website design work for your service's website. The good news is that getting a great-looking website can be very inexpensive because of the currently available applications.

Mistake to Avoid #16: Not Having Needed Technology

I was surprised that a few SBFs blamed the failures of the businesses they had started due to not having the right technology to operate efficiently.

Pro-tip: Identify the technology your business will need to compete and reflect the technology's cost in your business projections.

The reality is that your business will probably need to be adapting continuously to keep up with evolving technology. New technologies often force companies to adapt or die.

Mistake To Avoid #17: Poor Turn of Inventory

If you have inventory that isn't moving, you have another option beyond just sitting with the merchandise or pricing it so low that it sells. Consider joining a barter exchange.

One SBF commented that he was in business for a year before he learned he could have sold his excess product inventory for barter trade units from a barter exchange organization. He could also have used his inventory to buy goods or services his company needed from other barter exchange members using the trade units.

There is usually an initial fee to join a barter exchange, plus annual dues and a service fee on trades as they are consummated. Also, be warned: Bartering through an exchange is not a way to escape income taxes in most, if not all, countries. Barter units earned from sales less than the barter units you use to buy products and services for business purposes are taxable.

Mistake To Avoid #18: Customers Didn't Comply with Agreed Upon Payment Terms

Some SBFs said they had not been aggressive enough in collecting late payments for fear of losing customers. Instead of pursuing payment of their invoices, they used inaction when their customers failed to comply with their agreed payment terms. Their inactivity made customers believe they didn't have to pay on time.

So, aggressively follow up when payment dates are missed from the time you open for business. The lesson is: Ask for what is owed to you when it is owed.

Mistake To Avoid #19: Took Too Many Risks

Those who responded said they believed in their start-ups and their business models. As a result, a few of the SBFs who had previous businesses that failed blamed the earlier failures on making risky decisions with their belief that the risks were manageable. Unfortunately, they were wrong.

Their businesses would probably not have failed if they had spent more time analyzing situations and were more careful about taking business risks.

Mistake To Avoid #20: Too Slow to Make Needed Changes

Sometimes things in a start-up business need to be changed because things are not working as expected. It's common for start-up businesses to adapt to survive, and adjusting promptly is essential.

A few SBFs said their previous businesses failed because they were too slow to make needed changes to adjust to start-up business realities. Why would they wait? Often it was because they stubbornly wanted to prove that their initial business models worked.

When you begin your business, you will make mistakes. The trick is to learn from your errors and adapt as needed.

Conclusion

Don't get bogged down obsessing over mistakes made. Instead, maintain a positive, realistic attitude as you and your business adjust, evolve and grow!

Winners apply what they learned from their failures, grow, and move forward.

"If you are not wrong about some things, you're really wrong."

Media Mogul Barry Diller

Learn from the mistakes made by others with their start-up businesses. By knowing the mistakes that have hurt and sometimes even destroyed other start-up businesses, you'll recognize what you need to avoid. As a result, your start-up businesses will have an increased chance of survival and success.

PART THREE: YOUR SELF DISCOVERY

Are You up to the Challenge?

Welcome to Part Three, where you'll learn why you must conduct an honest, objective self-evaluation and how to do it. It's essential to know yourself before finalizing your decision to start a business and before selecting the kind of business you should start. But also to better understand whether you should be starting a business. After all, entrepreneurship is not for everyone.

Together, we'll review in Chapter Five the things you need to identify about yourself as part of self-evaluation. You will learn how to identify your Strengths, Weaknesses, Opportunities, and Threats that would be important to the new company you start.

In Chapter Six, you will learn how to create a written personal Vision Statement and use it.

Chapter Seven will examine why you have failed to start a business despite wanting to start a business. You will then learn how to overcome those barriers holding you back.

CHAPTER FIVE: SWOT EVALUATION

Introduction

But first, *slow down*, hard charger. As the British say, take a breath and "Have a think." Before finalizing your decision to start a business and selecting the company you want to start, take an honest "Look in The Mirror."

Shakespeare wrote, "To thine own self be true." But that can only happen if you recognize who you are. And forgive me for stating the obvious, but the best time to self-evaluate is *at the beginning of your process.*

Once you have completed the self-assessment questions, you will better understand your ability to do what's needed to start a new business. You may be surprised at the interesting things you discover about yourself.

He who knows others is learned.

He who knows himself is wise.

Lao Tse

It would be best if you took the time to look at yourself objectively before you decide that starting a business is right for you. Doing so will help you clarify the pros and cons of moving ahead. Your answers to the self-evaluation questions I will share will help you see things that could affect your desire to own a business.

If you decide that starting a business is right for you, the self-evaluation will help you decide what type of business is best for you to start. It will help you identify key business characteristics, such as the initial size, support staff, family-type vs. nonfamily involvement, and many other essential things in selecting the right business *for you to start.*

Many of the SBFs I spoke with said they were not happy being business owners. They had in common that the businesses they started did not fit them well. So take heed because selecting the right company to start is key to your long-term happiness.

So now, let's look at an easy way to analyze the personal strengths, weaknesses, opportunities, and threats that will significantly impact the results of any business you start. This kind of analysis is referred to as a SWOT analysis.

SWOT Analysis

The SWOT identifies your **S**trengths, **W**eaknesses, **O**pportunities, and **T**hreats. Doing a SWOT analysis is a relatively easy way to do a self-assessment. Any company you consider starting should fit your SWOT analysis. The SWOT survey will also help you decide on size, need for financing, and family involvement. Pick a business to start that will capitalize upon your strengths and not require you to be strong in an area that is a weakness for you. Doing this match will make you more likely to spend your time productively on your new business needs and enjoy your work!

Pro-tip: Never try to be someone you aren't.

After your self-evaluation, including your SWOT, you will know what you can accomplish by yourself and where you need help. You can't find the business that's the right fit for you if you don't have an objective evaluation of who you are. The results of your self-evaluation will go a long way in directing you to the right business for you to start.

Warning: Your self-evaluation exercise may not always be uplifting. Sometimes it may even be painful. But that is the point. Better to have the pain of honest realization versus the pain of delusion leading to a business failure later.

Although you may have a hard time with the self-examination, the exercise will lead you to a business that is right for you.

Your Strengths

Your strengths are your business advantage, which is the cornerstone for selecting the right business to start. So think of your strengths as your "Competitive Edges." It is essential to identify yours and then imagine how you can best use them by spending a lot, if not most of your business time using them at work. Equally important, when you spend a lot of work time using your strengths, you'll get more satisfaction from your involvement in the business.

Pro-Tip: The more percentage of your time you work involving your strengths, the more you will make a significant positive impact on your business.

Let's look at some examples of strengths of business founders that increase the chances of start-up companies succeeding.

Negotiating Skills

Some strengths will help you as the owner of almost every business. One is having negotiating skills. Unfortunately, many bright, talented people are simply bad as negotiators. They don't have the instinct for it and will probably never be outstanding at it. Some businesses require much more negotiating than other businesses. If being bad at negotiating sounds like you, you don't want to start a business where you would have to have strong negotiating skills. That is unless you have someone who can do your negotiating for you.

Whether they like it or not, business owners are responsible for some amount of negotiating. You might say that doing some amount of negotiating is a non-negotiable business activity for a business owner.

Even if this is very uncomfortable, there will be times that, as a business owner, you will have to negotiate with others, such as when you are:

- Negotiating leases for office space needed by your business
- Working out borrowing terms with a lender
- Requesting discounts from a vendor
- Requiring upfront payments from clients

  So, if there is a gap in your negotiating skills, you do need to try to learn basic negotiating skills. Let me share three guidelines that will help you to negotiate better.

- The first guideline is to *Think through your objectives and identify them before your negotiations*. Knowing your objectives helps you identify which issues are negotiable and those that are not. Giving in would destroy the chances of your new business succeeding. Your goals will clearly show you your ideal outcome from the negotiations.

- *The second guideline is to study non-verbal cues from the other side of your first offer. Your first offer is usually viewed as a starting point and seen as flexible rather than your final ask. Make sure you understand that dynamic before throwing it out there.*

- *The third is to understand the person's needs with whom you are negotiating. That way, you can frame your offer so that it solves the needs of the person with whom you are dealing.*

Specialized Knowledge, Talents, or Skills

But what about specialized knowledge, talents, or skills you have that may offer extra value in running a particular type of business? It will be helpful to the chances of your new business succeeding if you can capitalize on specialized experience, knowledge, talents, skills, or education.

If your new business involves areas in which you have expertise, knowledge (which may or may not be formal education), and contacts, that's almost like money in the bank!

For some businesses, specific strengths are helpful. For some other types of companies, it is closer to a requirement. Examples would be needed technical skills for owning an auto repair, relevant education to be a business advisor, or a specific type of experience and aptitude to become a decorator.

What recent experience do you have that you can use in the business that would be valuable to the needs of a new business you are considering? You don't want your company to fail, for example, because you pursued a business in a field that required a specific type of knowledge and for which you had little or no understanding.

If your new business is in a field where you have the background, your chances of succeeding go up. As a soon-to-be newly-hatched business entrepreneur, you should have some basic knowledge of certain start-up businesses, whether from previous business experience or a serious hobby. The more background you have in the type of business you want to start, the greater your chances of success in the industry.

So, give priority to a business that uses your work experience. Without your having a needed background for certain start-ups, they may turn into a quick wind-down business.

Remarkably, many executives have started businesses in fields with little or no knowledge of that field. Not surprising is that a large percentage of them failed.

While it is just an advantage to have industry knowledge for some businesses, it is needed for some other companies. So, if you are set on starting a business in which industry knowledge is necessary to succeed, you can work around the problem in several ways. You can hire someone with that required experience! Or, you can take a job in the industry for whatever time it takes to learn its nuances. Better to be prepared than to rush the process of starting the company.

A Case History: A couple of men discharged by their employer when the company was sold to a much larger concern came to me to discuss their desire to open a particular retail business, even though they were capable and experienced managers. They had visited a city where they had seen a specialized retail company not operating in their town and wanted to open such a retail store.

These men, however, had never been involved in the retail business and did not know what it takes to run a retail store! For example, they didn't know what it would cost to staff the store with personnel and products to sell. They also didn't know a lot about the products and costs of what they wanted to sell. No, I am not making this up. Fortunately, they decided that because of their lack of training and expertise in the business they were considering, it would be better to start a company that was more suited to their background.

But before you rule out starting a business for which you have no experience, consider the following:

- *Work for a company in a similar industry to learn* the ways of that business before you start your own. One SBF took a job with a baker and worked there for 18 months before opening a bakery at the other end of town
- *Take industry-specific online courses available to you from industry associations*
- *Research the industry in which you want to operate to understand its critical needs*

No matter how much research you do, the path to getting the knowledge you need for your new business, which you don't currently have, will probably not be perfect. So, don't create a paralysis-by-analysis situation. After you have picked a path, do what you can to get the knowledge that will make the ownership of the start-up easier for you to do successfully.

Passion

"Choose a job you love, and you will never have to work a day in your life."

The quote above has been attributed to Mark Twain, Confucius, or Marc Anthony. Well, whoever came up with the quote, I think he was exaggerating a bit, but only a bit.

But there is no denying that having a passion for a business is a valuable strength. Passion is the straw that stirs the drink, the key that turns over the engine, and the gas that keeps it running. If you enjoy the work, you will be more inclined to stick with things during the learning and trial-and-error phase that has destroyed businesses because the founders give up on the companies.

Using the area of passion has been a key for many successful start-up businesses whose founders started enterprises that involved their passions. In other words, they naturally gravitate towards areas they love.

What kind of business would involve your passion/calling? What things would make you want to go to work each day? What companies would provide you with psychic rewards? Do you have a hobby you enjoy that could be turned into a business?

If you have a passion for a business, you are also more likely to be willing to work harder than you have ever worked before. Make that *much, much harder* than you have ever before. Start-up business ownership is not easy. Forty-hour weeks? Fuggedaboutit! Those days are gone for a few years, at least. You'll probably need to be putting in 60 to 70 hours a week during the early years of the business. The funny thing is, if you pick the right company, you'll want to put in that time.

If you like what you do for a living, work feels less like a chore and more like an opportunity for achievement, growth, and fulfillment. It may be difficult, even disappointing, at times. But the drive comes naturally when you do what you love and do it in your own business. That's called passion.

Without it, you will be less likely to stick with things when they are not going well in the start-up phase. It will be easy to quit and move on to a job or start another business.

Are there emotional rewards you seek from your new business? Is there a product or service you want to provide because of the benefits? Many SBFs shared that they have passion for what they do. They shared how they get an emotional, psychic reward from the success of someone they have helped.

I can relate.

When I started TAB, I felt a great passion for creating something that would provide business owners with services to help them lead their businesses to tremendous success and help them to live more satisfying lives. TAB has been a passion that has brought me an immense psychological reward. Interestingly, many TAB franchisees, who are implementers of the system, have commented about their passion for providing TAB services to TAB members and how they enjoy seeing the positive difference it makes in their lives.

For many, their passion involves starting businesses that do what they have enjoyed doing as hobbies. It's interesting how often hobbies have turned into successful companies.

One of my friends worked for a company for a couple of decades before another company bought it, and he lost his executive job. He decided that the way to never again be at the mercy of an employer was to start his own business. His hobby, which he had done for years, involved helping friends finish their basements and other home improvement projects. He passionately enjoyed looking at projects when they were completed and knowing that he was the most responsible for how they came out.

So, he started a remodeling business incorporating his background, interests, and passion. The result was that the company achieved the level of success he wanted, and he enjoyed the experience of doing what he felt passionate about.

Identify what type of business you feel passionate about that motivates you and brings you joy, which may lead you to the business of your dreams.

Outstanding Special Aptitude

Many SBFs have areas in which they have outstanding aptitudes that have made a significant positive impact on their businesses. For example, one SBF had only a high-school education when he started his business. He sold the business several years later for millions. The key to his company's success was his selling gift.

He exploited his selling and powers of persuasion and "natural sizzle" as the primary focus of his activities in his business. He used his charisma. (As he loves being the center of attention, I suspect he would have been equally successful as a comedic actor or comedian.)

What Strengths do you Have

What strengths do you have that can increase the chances of making your new business successful? So, you must identify your strengths before selecting the right company for you to start. Try to use 100 words or less to identify your strengths in writing.

The following is an example of how one SBF identified viewed his strengths before he selected the business that he started:

- Willing to work long hours
- Creative
- Good at controlling expenses
- Able to excite employees
- Enjoys multi-tasking

Your Weaknesses

An old business adage calls ambition "the ingredient that makes dough rise." But ambition may not be enough to counteract weaknesses in experience, skills, passion, or the willingness to work long hours.

Until some situation or truth-teller exposes our shortcomings, many go blissfully through life, completely unaware of their weak points. Most of us do things how we've always done them, for better or worse, without thinking. Then, something hits the fan or a significant change, like starting a business, reveals our soft spots.

It's better to proactively look for an honest evaluation so that you are not vulnerable to the weaknesses you may have. So, be honest with yourself about your weaknesses that could impact the results of a business you want to start. Make a list of your weaknesses that you believe could hurt or prevent your start-up from succeeding.

As part of your effort to identify your weaknesses, consider the value of getting feedback from different sources, including your spouses, other relatives, and friends. Ask them if they would share what they see as weaknesses you have that could hurt or even prevent your start-up from succeeding. Make a list of all their responses.

Then compare both lists for any item repeated, even though it may appear in a different form or situation. Start with any weaknesses on both lists, and then decide how you can overcome the weakness so that it will not impede the success of your start-up.

The following are things identified by SBFs who went through the step of identifying their weaknesses before starting new businesses:

Limited Education Level

An excellent formal education level is valuable and may be essential to succeed in some businesses. But don't let a lack of formal education keep you from starting a business. For example, a friend of mine who left high school to join the military before he graduated high school started a used car business that eventually led to him owning several car dealerships.

Just look for a business that does not require formal education beyond what you have.

Bad Time Management Habits

Some SBFs identified being terrible at managing their own time as a weakness. The good news is that techniques are available to make your time management more effective if you want to overcome this weakness.

Impatience

Many SBFs acknowledged that they were impatient by nature. They had to force themselves to have the patience to take more extended views toward seeing results. The reality is that those who start businesses with get-rich-quick ideas are typically more likely to be the ones who fail. Launching and then owning a business is not like running a sprint. It is like running a marathon and requires at least a minim of long-term business patience.

Conflict Avoidance

Some people are very uncomfortable and, as a result, go out of their way to avoid conflict. This attitude about avoiding conflict can hurt your ability to lead a business.

Have you ever delayed or put off firing someone who hurt the company because you don't like conflicts? For many people, that's their normal, if self-defeating, response to a conflict situation.

Having a nature where you avoid conflict does not mean you should avoid becoming an entrepreneur. However, it does mean that you should consider a business that would limit your need to deal frequently with conflict resolution. There are some types of companies with fewer conflict situations than others. One type of business is a business with no employees to manage. You may need to set a limit as to the maximum number of employees you want your company to employ, such as that it should not exceed ten employees.

So ask yourself whether you shy away from resolving difficulties with other employees to avoid conflict. And if your answer is yes, how will you neutralize this weakness?

Become Too Close Friends with Direct Reports

Some SBFs identified their history of getting into close relationships with those who report to them as a weakness. Some people want to be liked, which leads them to befriend their employees when they should try to maintain a manager relationship with them.

And what happens then? They often do not manage their friends who report to them the same way they manage others. It includes allowing things to happen that should be unacceptable.

One SBF shared a story about an experience in the job she had before starting her business. She became close friends with another manager who reported to her. She even confided in the other manager regarding her family matters. Morale, with others who reported to her, was damaged because she allowed the manager/close friend to get away with things that would not be allowed to be done by others. She also gave the manager/friend choice assignments.

When discussing this weakness, she said that she knew that she should not and would not become close friends with any employees in her start-up.

Technology Phobic

Some SBFs listed their lack of technical skills and block in learning about technology as one of their weaknesses. Many bright, talented people are technology-phobic, which has not stopped their businesses from succeeding. However, it did cause their founders to either hire an employee to handle their companies' technology needs or engage independent contractors.

Too Involved in Things Outside of Business

Some SBFs identified a weakness of being involved in too many things outside the business. Owning a business will probably interfere with your non-work lifestyle. You need to be prepared to sacrifice until you can back off on the amount of focus your business needs from you.

One SBF said that before starting her business, she was so "involved in political/social activities that it distracted me from giving my work the focus it needed." Before starting her start-up business, she resigned from the boards of two different charities she had been on to have more time to focus on her start-up business.

Don't Want to Give a Personal Guarantee for Financing

Most start-ups require some level of outside financing. One woman listed one of her weaknesses as being risk-averse and explained that, as a result, she did not want to "put her personal assets at risk." She never obtained the loan she needed to start a business because the banks she went to required her guarantee to get the loan.

Starting a new business will typically require some initial investment, or loans, in the early stage of your company. How much are you – and your spouse, if applicable -- willing to guarantee personally to get a loan for the new business? How much collateral are you ready to pledge to get loans to your company?

If you don't want to give a personal guarantee for a bank loan for your start-up, consider other sources of financing that do not require personal security, such as borrowing from a relative. You may need a partner(s) in the business to get the company adequately financed.

You don't want to start an underfinanced business, which is a significant reason businesses fail.

History of Burnouts

Some people push themselves beyond reasonable limits. Their weakness is that they suffer burnout when they push themselves to the point where they exceed their physical and mental limits. Some people need to shut down and disengage when they reach their limits.

If business owners shut down and disengage, it hurts their businesses. When this happens, the odds are high that they will make bad business decisions and avoid making decisions that need to be made.

Burnout can be avoided, which could mean committing to doing something like taking an afternoon off each week or not taking on too much. These strategies can dramatically decrease the likelihood of burnout.

Need to Take Salary From the Business

Founders of most start-ups keep the amount of money they have the businesses pay them to a minimum. If you need an income level from the beginning, recognize it and decide how to deal with it. The salary may be for yourself to support your family, or you may feel you need to have family members employed in your business.

So, identify the minimum income you need to generate from your new business when it starts operating. Can you hold off taking out any money until the business has a positive cash flow? You may need to keep your current employment and income by starting the business part-time until your company grows to be enough to support you.

What Are Your Weaknesses?

Now, in 100 words or less, 'fess up! Write a Personal Weaknesses Statement that identifies the weaknesses that could have the most significant negative impact on your start-up business succeeding. Dig down and ask yourself if you have flaws that need to be addressed before starting a business.

Personal Opportunities

Do you see opportunities that could help your new business succeed if you could capitalize on them? Don't ignore things that might be opportunities but are so close, so common in your daily life, that you are, as the expression goes, "Not seeing the forest for the trees."

One SBF had been overweight for years and dealt with a body image disorder. The SBF "just got tired of looking dumpy and did something about it at a certain point." She improved her self-image by shedding over 50 pounds. The experience was so transformative physically and emotionally that the SBF felt she had found her calling. Realizing how much others could be helped by following the same program, the SBF decided there was an opportunity to start a business that shared what she had learned. She launched a fitness center for overweight women.

Another SBF for years had an interest in preserving a safe and healthy environment. His curiosity led him to learn about pollution abatement and handling hazardous waste. He recognized that he could use this knowledge as an opportunity to start a business that helped others with environmental protection, and the company he started did assist with helping the environment.

Sometimes there are opportunities due to relationships you may have. One SBF had a friend who was purchasing agent for a company that needed certain services that he could provide at competitive rates. He started a new company that provided these services, with his friend's company being his first client. His business transformed into a substantial business with many additional clients within a few years.

Once you have identified opportunities, describe them in 100 words or less in a written Personal Opportunities Statement.

Personal Threats

The "T" in SWOT refers to personal threats you need to consider that could negatively affect the success of the business you're thinking about starting. You cannot control these threats, but you can control how you react to them.

Many SBFs said they had identified one of their threats as health issues.

If you have a serious health problem, it should be considered when deciding whether you should start a business. It should also influence what kind of business you should start if you start a business.

One SBF feared that starting a business would exacerbate his high blood pressure. He noted that his high blood pressure gets very high when work is stressful. He decided to start a company with an assistant for him but no other employees because it would reduce management-related situations that could cause stress.

Another example of a threat was identified by another SBF, who was concerned that he might have to go through a "messy" divorce, which could sidetrack him from focusing on running a new business. He explained that he and his wife were separated before starting his business. He didn't want a divorce, but the decision was out of his control. Despite this situation, he decided to start a business. As he feared it would take place, his wife filed for divorce only months after starting his new business. Although the divorce proceedings negatively impacted his focus on his business, he got through the rough period, and his company ultimately succeeded.

Don't view all your current threats as etched in stone since, fortunately, many things change! Facts and circumstances in your life and business will inevitably evolve, and some threats will disappear.

Consider the most significant personal threats in your life that could negatively impact a business you start. Then write a personal threats statement that describes the threats in 100 words or less.

Conclusion

Doing your SWOT analysis will cost you nothing but your time and bring significant benefits. Once you've completed your SWOT "Look in the Mirror," you will have better insight into whether being a business owner is for you. After doing your SWOT analysis, you might decide that starting a business is for you, but you need to slow down your timing for when to start a business. Believe it or not, a delay may be good news. A delay may help you avoid big trouble down the road.

Also, as a result of a SWOT analysis, you may see the need to change course about what business to choose as a bonus. Gaining an in-depth understanding of yourself is necessary for selecting the right company to start that will bring you happiness and fulfillment.

KEY POINT: Once revealed, never let a misguided preliminary decision keep you on the wrong path. Pivot and persevere anew!

In addition to doing your SWOT analysis, consider taking an inexpensive personality/behavioral survey to give you additional information for your self-review. All you have to do is answer the questions asked by the survey. The survey company will then provide a written analysis of your natural personality/behavioral and adaptive styles. I prefer a survey based on the DISC (dominance, influencing, steadiness, and compliance) assessment model.

When you do your self-assessment, try to identify tasks that bring you joy and those that bore you. Likewise, try to identify the tasks for which you have solid skills and those for which you have weak skills.

The more you do things you enjoy and have natural solid skills for, the greater the likelihood your business will grow and bring you the fulfillment you desire. If possible, find others to do the tasks that bore you and for which you have weak natural skills.

CHAPTER SIX: PERSONAL VISION STATEMENT

Introduction

Your Personal Vision Statement (sometimes referred to as a "PVS") should reflect what you would like your life to be in five to ten years. Close your eyes and look ahead. That's not an oxymoron. Look ahead with your mind's eye and picture what you want for your life that will bring you happiness and fulfillment. Otherwise, why pursue the business?

Your Personal Vision Statement needs to be uniquely *yours.* It should be clear, simple, and realistically achievable. It needs to be completed before selecting the type of business you want to start so that the company you create is in alignment with your PVS. Picking a business that aligns with your PVS will save you from wasting your energy and financial resources by starting a company that's unlikely to help you attain the vision you want for your future.

What Factors Should be Considered

The following are some areas that involve business or work-related factors which you should think about when creating your Personal Vision Statement:

Business Revenue and Profits

What do you want the business success of your new business to look like five to 10 years in the future? It includes financial factors such as annual revenue and profits you desire your company to generate.

Financial Rewards you Want From the Company

What about the material rewards you desire to receive from the business so you can live the kind of lifestyle you like? It includes such things as income level and benefits that you want to receive. For purposes of your PVS, you should reflect the salary and benefits you want to take out from the business annually for five to 10 years.

NOTE: The income level and benefits in your PVS will probably differ from the income you need to take out of the business initially to support yourself during the company's early years.

Number of Employees

What number of full-time employees in the business would you like the company to employ five to 10 years in the future? Many dream of their companies having many full-time employees. Other business founders have started their businesses not to have to manage employees or, at most, only a small number of employees.

How many employees do you want to manage? Maybe a lot, perhaps a few, maybe one, perhaps none. There is no one correct answer for everyone, just an answer right for you.

The answer was clear for one of my friends who did not want "to own a business that would own him." He had previously managed large numbers of employees as an executive of a company. When let go by his employer, he decided to start a business where he could contract all the needed services.

Part-Time or Full-Time Business

It's estimated that 30 to 50% percent of business start-ups are started by founders who kept their jobs when they started their new businesses. For some founders, they want to stay part-time in the long-term future. They may have started their businesses to earn extra income, such as to help with expenses while raising children or to pay for their college education.

But for most, the dream is for the founders to be able to support themselves by being full-time involved in the businesses. These businesses, sometimes called "stepping-stone" start-ups, have founders who typically started the businesses while holding full-time jobs. They did it this way because they wanted the safety net of having a paycheck until their new companies grew to be able to support them. This stepping-stone approach is psychologically and economically crucial to these business founders because, in most cases, they feel they could not afford to give up the income from their full-time jobs when the businesses started.

Stepping-stone businesses permit the founder to take a "one foot in and one foot out" approach. The one-foot-in refers to keeping a full-time job while launching a company intended to become a full-time involvement in the future. Many stepping-stone businesses are initially operated out of a home office with no employees or just a small staff and typically only a limited amount of equipment.

One SBF started a part-time janitorial office service in which he worked only part-time until it generated enough revenue to replace the pay from his day job. When working part-time in the business during the early years, he did business development after regular working hours at his full-time job. He engaged independent contractors to do the janitorial work. When the business grew to generate enough revenue to replace the pay from his day job, he quit working full-time in his company.

KEY POINT: If your dream is for your start-up to be a stepping-stone business, create a business plan to help grow the company to a point where the business can support you full-time.

Stepping-stone businesses can become very big businesses. I enjoyed sharing the podium at an international business conference with a woman who invested $2,000 in products to start a part-time business. She said that she began the company at the age of twenty-four to supplement her family income. She worked out of her house, using her kitchen table to sort and fill orders. It became a full-time work commitment as it grew and sold for millions of dollars.

Your Work Activities

For most business founders, having a successful business alone is not enough to bring happiness. Happiness also depends on what the founders do in the business; their roles. Your PVS must reflect what you want to be doing in your business.

Here's good news, founder-to-be: As the business owner, you will control your role in your company. You will be among a small percentage of people who can create a job description for what you do at work tailored to who you are and how you want your daily work life to look.

Which begs the question: How do you want to spend your work time in your business? What role do you intend to play in the future for your organization? Ideally, these are the kind of activities and responsibilities that you will find enjoyable doing. So think about what works with the company you can do that you see as giving you the most pleasure in the long-term future.

Products or Services That Satisfy Personal Passion

Is there an activity, passion, cause, or hobby that is so important to you that you want it to be somehow involved in the long-term future of your start-up? For example, do you worry about the environment?

Every serious interest you feel passionately about is a potential business waiting to be launched. Imagine the energy you would bring to a company you control that reflects your passions and, simultaneously, could become a profit center. You would be spending your days in your field of dreams.

Partners

Do you envision having one or more partners with you in the business? If so, it should be reflected in your PVS. It will affect many of your decisions for your start-up.

But, before you have decided that your business would benefit if you had a partner, you will need to consider some things.

If you will have a partner, it is important who you select to be your partner. Running a profitable business while maintaining a happy and harmonious relationship can be a great joy, sharing the ups and downs with a supportive partner. A partner may have sounded like a good idea, but it may be a boneheaded mistake if you are not careful in picking who your partner will be and how your business relationship will look.

However, before you go too far down that path, consider this: According to the publication ICSTD, a USA business publication, "Partnerships fail about 80 percent of the time." Also, if you are considering going into a business partnership with a friend, think twice and thrice. Many collaborations with friends have ended friendships. Things can get ugly in a relationship when friends work together.

When looking into the future of who you would like to be partners with, consider whether your partner's skills complement yours or are redundant. Partners should bring something to the business that you don't have.

All partners must understand and accept their respective business responsibilities if they decide to have a partner. Knowing and accepting their roles and the work efforts expected of the partners will increase the chances of the partnership working long-term.

KEY POINT: It is best to have a formal written partnership agreement between you and your partner(s) that outlines the partnership's parameters and the partners' duties and obligations. The

partnership agreement governs such things as the management aspects, profit and loss distribution, and partnership dissolution. It includes the transferability of the partnership interest. Your Partnership Agreement should also have unambiguous buy-sell terms to protect the business from adversely affecting a partner's death, disability, or departure.

Ensure that your partnership agreement contains exit provisions if you have a partner. Think of it like a prenup, which looks ahead while everyone is still cordial, giving each party escape routes if the partnership is not working.

Balance Between Your Work Life and Non-Work Life

How do you want to balance your work and home (non-work) life long-term? Your PVS should identify a work-non-life balance that makes you happy. Identify the time you want to spend outside your business life doing personal activities that bring you happiness.

Include the amount of time you want to devote to the business weekly in your PVS. You might want to include periods for you not to be available for work to have the time to spend with family or other non-business-related activities.

The indispensable first step to getting the things you want out of life is this:

Decide what you want. Ben Stein.

Business owners have one of the biggest challenges balancing their personal and work lives. I've spoken with many SBFs whose businesses have made them multi-millionaires, yet they admitted they were unhappy. They've given a lot of reasons, including unhappy spouses, multiple marriages, and bad relationships with their children. Several of them felt that their lack of balance between their work and home life cost them their family relationships.

If you do not address your desired "balance of life" in your vision statement, you are not being honest with yourself. What impact do you want your new business to have on your personal life? Do you want your business and personal worlds to meld together, or are you happier keeping them separate?

Are you okay with being one of those business owners who miss out on their personal lives because they "don't have the time? Who is chained to work and so caught up in the day-to-day problems of the business that it leaves little time for anything else?

How important is it to take vacations or spend time with hobbies and pastimes? Here's a distasteful or exciting dose of reality: In most start-ups, the founder will probably work at least 50 to 60 hours weekly. How do you feel about that?

As a business owner, you will decide how much and when you work. Your days of blaming the boss for making you work late or not giving you time away from work are over, friend.

Your living is determined not so much by what life brings to you but by the attitude you bring to life; not so much by what happens to you as by how your mind looks at what happens.

-John Homer Miller

Exit Strategy

Do you want to sell the business if it achieves a specific market sale value within five or ten years reflected in the PVS? Some do not see or even want a clear exit point in their vision statement. On the other hand, some SBFs had told me that before their start-ups opened for business, they knew that they wanted to sell their within five to ten years and made decisions that they hoped would lead to them selling their businesses.

KEY POINT: Does your vision for your future include a stay-in or a get-out strategy?

In addition to the above point, ask yourself if other important factors should be in your PVS.

110

Conclusion

Your PVS will serve as a guide to help you identify the type of business that integrates with your long-term vision for what you want for your personal life. Only after you decide what you want for the future will you be able to identify the roadmap to create your ideal business and personal life.

But your PVS also provides you with a solid foundation to handle things. A business founder without a long-term vision of attainable dreams for the future is like a house without a solid foundation. When a tornado touches down, the trailer homes are often destroyed because they lack foundations. Your PVS is your solid foundation.

Once you have a clear personal vision for what you want your life to be five to ten years in the future, write it down as your PVS.

Before leaving this chapter, I want to point out that once you know the type of business you want to start, it is time to work on a Company Vision Statement that aligns with your PVS. The Company Vision Statement will show what you wish your start-up business to be in five to 10 years. It is sometimes referred to as a CVS.

Your CVS should reflect a vision that is realistically achievable and includes such things as:

- The primary products and services your company will offer and to whom they will be offered.

111

- The size you hope the company will be within a specific number of years.
- Geographic areas that the company will serve.

There is power in having a clear, exciting CVS that gets every employee aiming at the same target. Your CVS will help your employees make decisions. For example, before deciding to make a significant business expenditure, its merit should be weighed against its value in attaining your Company's Vision Statement.

There are other benefits to having a CVS in addition to providing direction to you and your employees. Your CVS keeps you're your business intact through the "storms," such as cash-flow challenges, losing customers, explosive growth, and staffing. Your CVS will also help you obtain financing and help recruit employees for your start-up business.

CHAPTER SEVEN: WHY HAVE YOU FAILED TO START A BUSINESS?

Introduction

"Hey, I know what we should do this weekend: Let's launch a business!" said no one *ever who has started a successful business!* People who start successful companies don't do it on a whim. Instead, they've been thinking about it for a while — often for years before taking the big step. And when they finally commit to starting their businesses, they're ready.

I developed a course for people who likely dreamed of starting their businesses. Everyone who took my course wanted to start a business. Why else would they have registered for the course on starting a business? And yet, when we conducted a follow-up survey two years later, only about 25 percent of them had started companies.

True, some should never open a business because they are not suited to become entrepreneurs. But most of them had the attributes, ability, experience, and skills needed to start a business and could have been successful business owners. So, in the short survey we sent out, we asked those who responded that they didn't start a business "why" they didn't become business owners.

What happened? Why did some take the leap of starting a business while others decided to bail? In this chapter, I'll share the findings and roadblocks they identified as to why they succumbed to inaction or jumping ship on the idea of starting a business. We will look at the roadblocks encountered and how you can overcome them if they stop you from starting a business.

Roadblock #1: Lack of Support From Spouse or Life Partner

Some SBFs surveyed did not move ahead with starting a business because of a lack of support from their spouses or life partners. There are different reasons for the lack of support.

An important one is because they can't get around the fact that your starting a business will significantly change your non-work family life. Their concern is based on reality because owning a business will dramatically impact your personal life. Your personal and business life will be entangled from the moment you start your own business. The focus and time on your business during the start-up and early stages will take your attention away from your non-business relationships. Among the most common regrets I hear from the founders of new companies is how they neglected their families while striving to make their businesses successful.

Another reason for the lack of support is financial. The income you generate will inevitably be tied to the success of your business. It is typical for a business founder to sacrifice income during the early years of a business so that the money taken out of a start-up business is kept to a minimum.

Is your spouse willing to sacrifice the amount of attention you'll be giving family members during the early years of the business? Is your spouse willing to sacrifice income during the early years of a start-up business?

If the answer is no to either question, there will be a potential conflict with your spouse or partner. Trust me when I say that things will be much harder for you if you start your businesses without the support of your spouse or partner. Conflict at home has caused many business founders to give up on their new companies prematurely, companies that could have been successful with more time.

You must discuss with your spouse or life partner whether you have support to start a business and will that support continue if things don't go as well as you expected. You don't want a situation in which you will be second-guessed and your life miserable if things do not start well with your new business.

Getting support is essential. If you don't have the support of your spouse or life partner to start a business, your life could become miserable if things do not progress as well as you expected. On the other hand, having family support for what you are doing provides you with the emotional backing to manage anxiety when things do not go as expected in business. Fortunately, my wife, Judi, was totally supportive of my starting TAB.

So what can you do to bring about this support if you are experiencing this roadblock? Set aside time for the two of you to meet and discuss the situation openly.

At the meeting, discuss with your spouse or life partner how starting a business will hopefully lead your family to a happier life. Point out how it could result in less overall stress if the company becomes successful and allow the family to enjoy what they want in their lives.

Discuss that if you start the business running, it can cause stress and exhaustion for you. In more extreme situations, health problems can interfere with personal relationships, including time with the family.

Acknowledge that many business founders find that their businesses became the primary purpose in their lives during the early years of their companies but that you will try not to let that happen with you. Explain that you will try to keep the business from becoming an obsession, but there may be times to make notes of business-related challenges when you are at home. Be honest that your personal and business life will overlap. Explain that you can't change that, but you will try to keep the overlap in control.

You don't want to have the same experience as that of one woman who told me that her preoccupation with her business was the cause of her divorce from a man she loved.

KEY POINT: To understand how being a business owner will interact with your personal life, picture a Venn Diagram of two overlapping circles. One circle represents your personal life; the other is your business. The overlapping area is that part that combines them. The more closely the owner is involved with the company, the more significant the overlap. It's common for this overlap to be quite sizeable during the start-up and early stages of owning a business.

Roadblock #2: Negative Feedback Advice From Others

Let's say you're like most people considering starting a business. You'll probably ask non-spouse family members, friends, and business acquaintances for their input. You may need to have a few soul-baring dialogues with one or more of them because they are people whose advice you respect. Many who thought about starting a business, and didn't follow through, were listening to and following the feedback advice from others.

Once you reach out, you'll probably receive a lot of well-meaning counsel that you'll need to filter out. Be prepared to hear negative feedback about why you can't accomplish what you want with the new business. Poor timing. To much risk. Too much competition, and on and on.

If you ask for input from other advisors, don't lead the advisor by asking for information in a way that leads to a false endorsement of your decision. Don't ask if you're not looking for the truth. Be prepared for harsh feedback. Respect that they are sharing what they believe. The worst reaction you can display is defensiveness. If you get advice contrary to your belief, don't discredit it because you disagree with it. Your friends who share views you disagree with are probably just trying to help you. They don't want to see you hurt by starting a business they think might fail.

But be careful; *keep an open mind*. The likelihood is that some of the advice will be useful and should be considered when you decide. However, if you don't filter out the bad advice, it will lead you to the wrong choices. You must evaluate the value of the advice you receive before letting it stop you. Spend time deciding whether there is merit and whether or not it is helpful. Remember: When you ask for objective feedback, it's still your call regarding the weight you give it.

Also, consider who is giving the advice. For example, most people are not risk-takers. Ask yourself if the person giving the advice has an entrepreneurial mentality that accepts the risk of starting a business.

When I shared my thoughts about starting TAB with friends and business acquaintances, they advised me not to start TAB. They explained why they thought it would fail. I listened but then decided to ignore the advice of my friends and business acquaintances. If I had listened to their advice, TAB would not exist.

Roadblock #3: Fear of Failing

Risk is a natural byproduct of starting a business. There is a natural resistance to the risks associated with the big step of starting a business. When faced with whether to keep a secure job, many choose "job security." The fear of failure stops them in their tracks, and they don't take the steps needed to start a business.

Many come up with excuses not to move ahead with starting a business because doubt and indecision related to the fear of failure freeze them in place. Instead, they hide in their comfort zone of false security. They become victims of their unwillingness to take associated risks.

Let's be honest. Business start-ups often fail. So, it's okay to be afraid of failing, so long as the fear is not *so intense* that it stops you from trying. If you are in a holding pattern because of a fear of failure, don't lose sight of the great benefits if your start-up business succeeds.

But that's what separates the talkers from the SBFs who are doers, is that the. SBFs realize the risks associated with their businesses but overcome the fear because they want what will happen when their start-ups succeed. This desire empowered them to get started. It gave them the sense of urgency to take action.

If you are experiencing this roadblock of fear of failure, weigh the pros of what will happen if your start-up business succeeds against the negatives, including all the downsides if it doesn't work. Then consider the consequences of not starting up a business.

An example of a consequence may be that if you give up on pursuing your dream of being a business owner, you will fail to improve your circumstances. The result might be that if you don't act, you will probably experience the dread of regret for failing to act. So, weigh the cost of your inaction.

After identifying the pros and cons of starting a business, take some time to evaluate what would make you comfortable taking on this risk. Try to create a strategy that will keep the risk to a minimum. Then look at the picture again and decide if the fear of failure should be holding you back.

Roadblock #4: Inability to Compete Against Established Competition

The roadblock that caused some to scrap their start-up dreams of starting businesses was a concern about being able to compete with the established competition. They felt they could not contend with established competitors.

While this concern may be valid for some businesses, it is not true for all businesses. Just because your company is the small kid on the block doesn't mean you can't compete with the big boys. While this differs from the industry, the fact is that small privately-owned businesses have proven they can successfully go up against the competition. Start-up businesses have proven to compete against large companies, the established "Goliaths" in almost every industry.

But you can't beat them by playing their game. To compete successfully against the established competition, you'll need to identify and understand your competitive advantages and develop plans to use them.

Let's look at some of the competitive edges that your start-up business might have versus much larger established enterprises:

- *You can react faster than larger businesses.* Your start-up business can act quickly, responsibly, and decisively with you at the helm. You report only to you! As the owner, you can be more responsive to challenges without getting a consensus of executive-level views to make a decision. You will be able to call the shots promptly and with flexibility. In contrast, large companies often have several levels of communication that a plan must wend its way through before implementing changes. Start-up businesses have been better at responding to shifting needs in the economy and changes in trends because they can move faster to take advantage of changes in trends.

- *You can be more aggressive.* Large companies often foster a lack of bold action rooted in a management philosophy of not taking risks that could endanger their jobs. In contrast, you can take chances because you don't have to be concerned with the results affecting your career. As a business owner, you don't need to protect yourself from the fallout with a boss if your aggressive decisions turn out poorly. If you see something that needs to be done for your company, you can do it.

- *You are not as likely to be negatively affected by corporate politics and "backbiting."* The giant companies of the business world can't eliminate politics, and company politics often results in missed opportunities. Corporate politics is part of the nature of executives in all major companies." In contrast, as a business owner of a start-up business, you will make your decisions without considering company politics. If you see political games taking place, you can nip it by taking immediate action to eliminate politics at play.

- *Innovative.* Small businesses tend to be more creative because their owners often view their businesses as their "babies" and are the driving forces in their businesses to innovate as needed to compete.

While it does not give you a competitive advantage, other things will make it easier for start-up businesses to compete. One thing is that even small businesses have access to low-cost technology today, once available only to large companies. For example, you can access critically important market research information for marketing and engage various online services at affordable prices. You can find inexpensive and quality printing and graphic design services with fast turnaround times.

Other things you have available for businesses in many business fields are joining a buying group to buy materials and products at prices competitive with what established companies are paying. These groups help small and medium-sized businesses buy products at the same low prices as large businesses by pooling the group's purchasing power. Buying groups also allow business owners to have a private label or proprietary products, which would be difficult for most small and medium-sized businesses to have on their own. The advantage of private label products is that it makes it harder for a purchaser to compare prices. Another advantage of being a buying group member is that members have industry-specific discussions that improve the operating efficiency of the members.

Roadblock #5: Not the Right Time to Start a Business

Some avoided starting a business because "It's not the right time in my life to start a business?" Only a fool would say that timing is not essential. And if you're reading this book, you're no fool.

Timing is vital for when to take the giant leap of launching a business. The challenge is determining when is the right time. Things are constantly changing in the business world. Every decade products or services come to market that did not in the previous decade. Whether you should start your own business may change based on changing factors in your life that allow you to see things differently than in the past.

But don't wait to start your new business until you feel you know everything you can before beginning the business. Don't be one of those people who think they need to do more research, and then more, and then more! If you let this be how you approach it, you may never take the step you need to start your business. Don't let paralysis by analysis stop you.

Do you feel that owning your own business will give you something that may have been missing in your life? Do you have a great desire to strike out independently and become financially independent by starting a business, it is a sign that you are ready.

However, factors may temporarily stop you from starting a business. Identify them and be ready to act when they are resolved. Do the actions suggested in this book to guide you in selecting the right company to start and know what you need to do for launching the business, such as arranging for financing. You will be ready to move ahead when the factors holding you back are resolved and it is the right time for you to start your business. For example, one man's triggering event was when his children had all left home or graduated college. He only started the company that he had thought about for years.

Roadblock #6: Age

Some did not start their businesses because they felt they were too young or old to start a business. Hogwash! If you're ready for it, your age shouldn't stop you. Neither youth nor older age should keep you from converting a good idea, hobby, pastime, or passion into a successful business.

Millions, young and old, have successfully opened businesses that brought them a good income, happiness, and meaningful life. The age for when someone should become a business owner depends on when each individual to ready for the role.

Based on when TAB members became business founders, age is irrelevant. The average age range of TAB members when they started their businesses is 34 to 42 years old. However, some greatest success stories have come from younger SBFs, many starting their businesses in their 20s. Likewise, there are great success stories with others who were well past middle age, even in their 60s or older, when they started their businesses.

Consider Col. Harland Sanders, who started Kentucky Fried Chicken at age 66. Sanders went out on the road in his 70s and arranged for more than 600 franchises over nine years. Sanders bragged about how he had taken a pastime and turned it into wealth and satisfaction for himself. It made others financially independent who used his system, recipes, and techniques.

Roadblock #7: Health Issue

Some who dream of starting a business have not done so because of health issues. Do you have physical or mental health problems that have prevented you from moving forward? If so, consider whether there are types of businesses you could start where your health issue would not keep you from enjoying the experience of being a business owner.

Sometimes, you should delay starting the business until the health issue resolves itself or can be controlled. For example, if you are battling a mental illness such as depression, you may want to delay starting your business until you can manage how it affects you. Many SBFs with

126

mental issues have been able to work through the anxiety and stress. Someone with fear, for example, may not be able to eliminate the anxiety but has been able to deal with the stress and unexpected challenges that commonly occur during the early years of a business.

In addition to the more common reasons given above, some other reasons for not starting a business included the following.

- Did not want to make the needed sacrifice of generating less income in the early years of the start-up business than being paid at current employment and decided instead to "stay put" with their current job.
- Felt she could not get financing for the type of business she wanted to start. I have devoted a chapter on funding later in this book.
- She decided that her lack of a college-level education made her unprepared to start and run a business. Well, I'm here to tell you that this is a misconception. Yes, a college degree or formal education may be needed for specific companies. Still, many have created successful businesses in different fields without a high school diploma or a college degree.

Conclusion

What roadblock(s); have stopped you from launching your business start-up? Lost opportunities to start a business in the past should not rule out starting a business now. So, write down what has stopped you from becoming a business founder. Then ask yourself how you can overcome each of the roadblocks you identified.

If you decide to make starting your business a reality and currently have a job, don't notify your current employer of your intent to leave your job until everything is "nailed down." If you give notice before you have all your ducks in a row for starting the business, you could find yourself without having the paychecks you need from your current job or the new company.

PART FOUR- SELECTING THE BUSINESS TO START THAT BEST FITS YOU

You should have a good idea of who you are, what you would like your life to be in the next five to 10 years, and what has held you back. These are all important factors you should consider when picking the business that is the best fit for you to start. But there are other factors you need to consider. These factors are covered in Chapter Eight, which focuses on things you should consider when selecting the business that will be right for you to start. In Chapter Nine, you will learn things that will help you decide whether you want to choose a business to employ your family members.

The selection process is all about you. It's all about the fit. The same business that can energize one person can be enervating to another. The better the fit between the type of business you select, the greater the chances of it being successful.

CHAPTER EIGHT: SELECTING THE RIGHT BUSINESS FOR YOU TO START

Introduction

Every new business confronts unexpected challenges, and new business owners feel frustrated when things go poorly. Most new business owners will experience aggravation and headaches at the beginning of the operation of the business. So count on it happening to you.

But if you have chosen wisely the right business for you to start, it will be worth it because the level of frustration, aggravation, and headaches be reduced. You will love owning your business, and it will bring you enough joy to make the difficult times worth it.

When selecting the right business to start, you need to consider what you have learned about yourself in your self-evaluation when reading Part Three. But you should also consider the following other factors when determining the type of business that best fits you:

Your Passion for the Business

Although each SBF described it differently, the theme of successful business founders was the same: they were so passionate they had to fight against becoming obsessive about making their new businesses, which they loved, succeed. Many referred to their being obsessive about their businesses succeeding.

When you start a business that matches what you love to do and feel passionate about, you will be more motivated to make your business succeed. When you feel such passion, you will be happier as a business owner and rarely feel complacent or bored.

Passion for what your business provides its customers or clients will push you through the typical obstacles most start-ups face. Your passion will be like a "calling" that provides you with a hunger for your new businesses to succeed and will give you a driving force for improving and growing your business. You will always be looking for possibilities to improve your company.

Conversely, good luck if you feel no emotional connection to what your start-up business offers. Without it, you probably won't have the hunger to adapt, evolve, and build your business to its maximum potential.

Most SBFs who started businesses aligned with their passion interests said they were generally happy. In contrast, those who selected companies to start based only on the ability of the business to generate wealth but for which they had no passion were often unhappy business owners.

Your passion may be for the products or services a business will provide. It may be because they match the strong values that they represent. For example, some SBFs were passionate about positively impacting society or their community and selected businesses that help make that happen.

Many successful SBFs have created companies that did things that are meaningful to them. For example, one SBF has a strong passion for improving the environment. He started a business that was ecology-based. Your passionate belief in causes will give you additional motivation for your new business to succeed if it helps causes in which you have a strong belief.

The passion may involve lifestyle. Give extra weight to selecting a start-up opportunity that supports your desire for a type of lifestyle. One SBF had a passion for traveling. He started a business that packages group travel, enabling him to do a lot of international travel.

My passion for helping business owners become successful played a big part in why I founded TAB. This passion helped me persevere and make changes that led to the excellent success TAB has experienced worldwide. Many TAB franchise unit owners have told me they are implementers of the TAB system because they are passionate about seeing their members benefit from the TAB experience.

What businesses could you start that would satisfy one or more of your passionate interests and are also good fits with what you enjoy doing? Is there an area of business with products or services you enjoy and about which you feel passionate? Your passion might involve your favorite hobbies, travel activities, sports, etc. That, future business founder, is gold you should consider mining.

Your Role in the Business

Starting a business with a role you enjoy can differentiate between success and failure. So, ask yourself if, upon waking up, you'd be excited by the kind of work you would be doing in the business you're considering. Or if simply thinking about the challenges you might face in that business fills you with dread.

So, what type of business might allow you to have a role that involves what you enjoy doing? It's more likely you will be happy if your company role consists of doing what you enjoy.

If you don't enjoy doing the things you will be doing in the business, it will not fulfill your motivational needs, and the chances of success diminish. You will likely feel unfulfilled *even if the company is successful*.

One SBF called what he does in his business in a typical day as determined by "what do I want to be doing when I get to work each day." And he loves that role. You want to look in the mirror almost every morning and know that running your business is what you would like to do that day, even if

133

what you do may be so routine that it would make others very stressed or put others to sleep.

You will have to do things initially in your business that will not need to be an essential part of your role. So, don't eliminate viable businesses because of what you will have to do initially in your business if you won't have to do those things in the long run. In most new companies, you will.

Don't end your evaluation with start-up responsibilities that you may not enjoy. Look ahead and peer down the road for your future role rather than expecting a total fit initially. Over time, will you be able to move your activities into the role you want in your business?

You shouldn't rule out a business because your role in it will be similar to what you have been doing in your current employment. Many SBFs have started businesses that allowed them to enjoy a role, although the work might be similar to or the same as what they did in their previous job. The difference is that they are no longer doing it with the oversight of a boss and, instead, working for themselves.

The business you select should have a role for you that is within your comfort level for confrontations. The company you are considering starting should allow you to avoid doing what you hate most. Knowing your comfort level or discomfort with specific roles is vital to evaluating what kind of businesses will provide you with a role within your comfort zone.

For example, if you hate confrontation, consider businesses in which the owner's role does not have a lot of conflicts to handle with employees, vendors, customers, or clients. A man who had been a senior executive with a company with hundreds of employees acknowledged that he didn't like confrontations. He was always uncomfortable having disagreements with employees. So, we identified a business he could start from his house without him having to hire employees other than a part-time assistant.

You want to select a business to start that will make you happy operating it for the next ten years or more. So, consider what companies you could start that you think you would enjoy running for the next 10-plus years.

Work/Personal Life Balance

Your new business should match the lifestyle you want. If you're going to spend a certain amount of time with family or pursue personal activities, you'll need a business that allows it.

One business founder started a bakery. He opens his store early in the morning, but the trade-off is that he has free time later in the day for non-work-involved activities. He uses some of this time to play tennis a minimum of three times a week. Working the early hours was a compromise he could live with because it allowed him to have the life balance he wanted.

Part-Time Versus Full-Time Business

Do you want to start a small business with a part-time dedication to it to supplement your income, or do you want to start a full-time business with a full-time work focus? Companies that can be successfully operated by people part-time are generally easy to enter. Many of them can be tried part-time before you make a long-term full-time commitment to managing them.

To find part-time business start-up opportunities, shop for them the same you shop for anything else in the 21st Century: Surf the internet to find great research resources. Numerous websites will help you learn more about part-time

If a part-time business is what you want, do you want to operate it as a home-based business? Some SBFs selected businesses that could be started at home. They liked the fact that working remotely from home offered flexible work hours. Some liked that it allowed them to raise their children and still earn income. For many part-time businesses, running it from a home office gives flexibility regarding when and keeps down the overhead. For others, avoiding an office commute was important.

Whatever their reasons, technological advancements have made it easier than ever before to start home businesses. The barriers to entry are low. Using apps like Zoom and Skype, you can conduct virtual meetings with potential customers and clients around the globe from a bedroom or garage. You can get information through Google. You can market your product using an inexpensive website. You can order the products and materials you need as easily as an online meal. In other words, technology allows you to work from home with nearly anyone anywhere.

Operating a business from home doesn't have to be done with a plan to go from a part-time to a full-time business. Many companies have been launched from the founders' homes without intending that their businesses ever be more than a part-time activity. For example, a friend of mine was an executive of a company but had a side business of buying prestige brand cars that didn't run well. He installed the needed parts at night or on the weekends, did the repairs, cleaned them up, and sold them for a profit.

Your Expertise

When starting a business, it helps to have industry-specific experience and skills in the specific sector of the business. For some companies, it is essential. For others, it is not crucial. If experience is not necessary, you can often overcome your lack of expertise by investing the time to get exposure to the new business before you start the business.

What you do best is what you will want to do every day. So, what type of businesses will have you excelling daily? For most people, their work efforts naturally gravitate towards areas that come naturally, and they don't enjoy doing what there are not good at doing. If the work is natural for you and you enjoy doing it, it will generally be less stressful and more rewarding. For example, for those who are not good at managing others, there are start-up opportunities that do not require employees or just one support employee.

We are all good at certain things and bad at other things. Whatever business you have in mind should capitalize on what you do well. Likewise, it should not be dependent on you doing what you do poorly. For example, you may have a natural management aptitude. If so, don't rule out starting a business that requires you to manage employees just because you don't have management experience.

If you have a "Selling Personality," certain types of businesses will allow your skills to shine. On the other hand, if you are a technophobe, you will probably not be great with technology. So, starting a business in which the primary products or services are highly technological would probably be a bad idea.

What are you good at doing? When a friend of mine was from his executive position, he considered that he was very good at helping his friends and neighbors with their home improvement projects. He started a home remodeling company, which, if you'll excuse the pun, he "built" into a thriving business that reached the level of success he wanted.

Need That Isn't Being Served

Do you have a new service or product that you want to bring to market? Do you have a business idea that excites you? Your belief in your concepts could be the driving force that gets them over the finish line. But for sales of the new product or service to happen, there must be a demand for it.

Start-ups that sell products or services in search of demand are risky investments. It is much less risky, with chances of success escalating when there's a clearly-defined market with a strong need for the product or service. Sometimes there are demand trends, but question whether the trend has legs if you see such a trend. Some trends can change abruptly, burning out as fast as they catch fire.

An SBF's husband had died of alcoholism, and then her son began having drinking problems. Because she did not like the available treatment options, she came up with alternative treatment methods. Her approaches yielded highly positive results. She wanted to launch an alcoholic rehabilitation center that used her alternative treatment methods. After deciding the need existed, she started her rehab center, which became very successful.

If your prospects don't know they need your offering, you may be rolling a rock uphill. Few businesses that require stimulating the interest of an unaware or disinterested audience succeed quickly enough for the owners to turn a profit. After you are satisfied with the demand, ask yourself if your product or service can fulfill that need at a price that will allow you to make money.

Desirability of a Business

The least desirable businesses can often provide the most incredible opportunities to start. Question: Do you care if the company you launch would be undesirable to most people? Let me share some examples of people who started businesses that many consider undesirable. They started companies that would be unlikely to excite most people but were perfect fits for those who created them.

- A woman, bored with her clerical job, opened a company that did residential maid services and commercial cleaning. She enjoyed running the business even though many might find owning such a business "beneath them."
- A friend of mine launched a trash hauling business that became very successful.

These people were primarily concerned with income potential and did not care intensely about the personal image of owning those types of businesses.

For many others, it is vital to select a business to start that provides the prestige they want. It is widespread among those from senior executive positions who wish to mention at cocktail parties and other social gatherings that they own types of businesses that sound impressive.

The prestige factor is also related to the size they hope the business will become. Some look for companies with the chance to be viewed with the prestige coming from becoming very large, even global, in size.

Products or Services

Some select businesses sell products. These types of companies generally require significant investments in product inventory. However, there are some businesses where you can sell products without upfront inventory costs or shipping logistics. They involve dropping shipping and products sent directly from your wholesaler to your customers.

Others want to start businesses that offer services. Some pick a company to start that involves a service that the business founder has a skill level in providing. Some select service businesses to start because they do not require inventory. As a result, less capital is typically needed to start a service business than one that sells products.

Conclusion

Picking the right business for yourself requires a balance of emotion and passion with reason and cold logic. In short, don't pick a company that is a bad fit for you and is likely to turn out poorly, putting you in situations that may take years to unravel.

Consider what you learned about yourself from your self-evaluation when selecting a business to start. Embrace the factors you identified in your SWOT and what you want in your future that you specified in your PVS to deliver fulfillment and happiness. Consider what has stopped you in the past from starting a business.

Then determine your position on the several factors in this chapter to help you identify the best business to start. Once you select the business, you will need to determine if you can finance the new business. If you can't fund your first choice, be flexible. Select another type of start-up that requires the amount of financing you can provide or arrange to get.

The key is not to procrastinate. As the cliché says, time is money. You don't want to rush your selection, but you can't wait forever. It would be fantastic if you did not have to decide what business to start until you had all the information about the alternatives you are considering. Unfortunately, you will probably never have all the information you want. So decide on the type of business you should start and move forward.

CHAPTER NINE: SELECTING A BUSINESS THAT WILL EMPLOY FAMILY MEMBERS

Introduction

In addition to all businesses' challenges, family businesses face additional unique challenges. You can find a lot about family businesses in my book "9 Elements of Family Business Success." But, whether or not you read that book, there are some things you need to know about the dynamics of a family business before selecting a business that allows you to employ family members.

Working with family members can result in great satisfaction, but only if handled properly. And, even if handled properly, there will inevitably be both joy and frustrations from owning a family business.

Whether or not you have a family business and how you handle it, if you do, will be a significant factor in determining the quality of life for you and your family. So take the time to understand the ramifications before selecting a business employing one or more of your family members.

So, now let's look at some of the things you need to consider before selecting a business intended to employ family members.

Objectives in A Family Business are Often Different

In a company without family members as employees, business decisions are typically made to deliver better profit returns for the owner(s). In contrast, the objectives of family businesses typically differ from non-family firms. They make decisions that do not maximize the company's profits for the owner(s) but satisfy something related to the family.

Many, if not most, owners of family businesses define success as including things *in addition to profit*. They measure success for their companies in part based on the benefits provided to family members who work as employees. As a result, decisions in family businesses may be made to create jobs for family members even if they are not the most qualified for the jobs. Often family members will be given management positions when others should have been promoted. Sometimes family members will be employed even when there is no business need for them to be on the payroll.

If you are starting a family business, decide if your objective is to run the new company for maximum financial success or profits and family benefits. You can't have both. When you decide, you owe it to every family member you are considering hiring to let them know your company vision and how you intend to address the family member employee benefit versus maximizing profits factor in your company.

Family Business Miseries

Potential misunderstandings can make running a family business a nightmare. There are often significant conflicts when the business owner balances what is best for the family or individual relatives versus what is best for the business. Founders of family businesses often make decisions that are best for family relationships and not based on what is best for the company.

Be prepared to see that your business decisions in your family business may negatively impact your relationship with your family members. They may also negatively impact company results, resulting in the business underachieving in sales and profits.

Family member employees are not just like other employees. It's far more difficult for most business founders to supervise them impartially. The result, all too often, is that family member employees are managed differently than non-family member employees. When this happens, it negatively affects the company culture and the efforts of other employees in the business.

It also brings about stress from managing employees who are your family member. Managing family member-employees can ignite and fray family relationships with relatives. When they're unhappy with things at work, it is common for them to vent at home about the situation. This venting is one more reason that damaged family relationships take place.

Let me share only some of the many stories of family business miseries I could share with you.

The son of an SBF was doing shoddy work as a manager. He didn't seem to care, and many employees noticed this in the business. A few non-family member managers requested a meeting with the founder. They explained that his son's behavior was dragging down the company's morale, and they wanted the boss to either fix it or fire his son.

The father was aware that the son had a gambling problem. He felt that it was the cause of his son's poor work performance. He met with his son and gave him an ultimatum: Stop gambling or be fired. But the son did not stop gambling, and the SBF fired him.

As a result, the SBF's wife gave the SBF an ultimatum of her own. Until the founder rehired their son, she would not talk to or cook for him. And if that wasn't bad enough, the SBF's son's wife and three young children stopped talking to him.

Sad and conflicted (and maybe hungry), the founder relented. He hired back his son. The reaction from other employees was negative and swift. Within six months, three of his key managers quit the business.

Another SBF shared a challenge he had involving his wife, who was the CFO of his company. He said she was a good bookkeeper and a big help when his small business was small. But, the business had significantly grown. She was unqualified as an accountant and incapable of doing the CFO job. As a result, the accounting department employees resented reporting to her. Whenever he brought up the subject of her leaving the company, her response was "dramatic and unpleasant" for him.

The owner's son, the executive vice president of a distribution company, shared how frustrating it was for him and how bitter his feelings were because his father had made his youngest brother the company's sales manager. He explained that his brother was "barely qualified to manage himself, and now he oversees our sales staff of eight salespeople."

Before the promotion was announced, the son expressed his concerns to his father. His father responded that he was promoting his brother because 'he's a very good son, husband, and father." His father added, "as long as he gets adequate results, I'll leave him in the position." Within three months of the promotion announcement, the well-qualified employee who should have been promoted quit the company.

The founder of a nursing-aid home service started with a three-person management team that included her daughter and two experienced nursing-aid managers. Her daughter had no management experience and, in addition, no experience in the nursing-aid industry. The daughter made management decisions during the first few months that hurt the start-up business. The founder of the company decided that she had to fire her daughter. When she fired her daughter, it didn't exactly help the relationship between her and her daughter.

My last family business misery story involves an executive, the son-in-law of an SBF. He consistently came in late to work and sometimes failed to attend some meetings in which he was supposed to participate. The SBF decided to meet with his son-in-law to discuss his lack of accountability. The SBF warned his son-in-law that it had to stop during the meeting. And the problem stopped for a few months. But then, unfortunately, it started happening again.

So, the SBF had another meeting with his son-in-law, during which time he told his son-in-law to find another job if he continued not showing up on time and missed meetings scheduled for him to attend. The son-in-law did not wait and found a job shortly after the meeting. The result was a damaged relationship with his son-in-law, daughter, and wife.

Conclusion

Before you launch a family business start-up, try to anticipate how you would address the unique challenges of the family dynamics in the business and your personal life.

Think long before you hire family members for your start-up business. (It is your company, after all). If you select a family business to start, determine which family members *you want in the business* working for you and what roles they will play.

How you handle the family business dynamics will be a significant factor in determining your quality of life and that of your family, both employed and not employed by the business.

PART FIVE: SHOULD YOU START A BUSINESS BY BUYING A FRANCHISE?

The chances of your franchised business becoming successful are significantly increased if you are committed to following the franchisor's systems. This means that you must be comfortable following what the franchise system says you need to do to run the business, including using the system's processes, tools, etc., of the system.

Being part of a franchise system eliminates the need for you to do and create many things needed to start and run your business.

In this Part Five, you will learn about the many benefits of owning a franchise, the requirements imposed on franchisees on how the franchisees operate their businesses, and the upfront and launch time franchise-related costs you will need to incur if you buy a franchise.

CHAPTER TEN- PROS OF OWNING A FRANCHISE

Introduction

There are many benefits of owning a franchise that are "Pros." Let's look at some of the most important benefits of owning a franchise that helps explain why a franchised business has a much greater likelihood of succeeding.

#1: Less Risk of Failure

Starting your business as part of a mature franchise system is much easier and less risky than starting a business from scratch. Why? Because most of the unknowns should have already been eliminated by the time you buy your franchise.

No — owning a franchised business is not a guarantee your start-up business will be a success. Your odds of success rise exponentially compared to starting a business from scratch. And for that reason alone, you might want to consider starting your new business as a franchisee.

Let's look at some statistics that point out the difference in risk. It is estimated that fewer than five percent of franchisee-owned businesses are discontinued each year, and less than twenty-five percent of franchised units fail within that critical first five-year maturation threshold. In contrast, *about sixty-five percent of business start-ups that are not franchisees (sometimes called "start-ups from scratch") fail within five years.* Let me put this another way to drive the point home: Most new franchises survive the five-year mark, and most start-ups from scratch do not.

This risk factor needs to consider the maturity of the franchise system. A significant percentage of all new franchise systems that fail will do so within 12 years of the franchisor starting to franchise. So, the risk of buying a franchise increases if the franchisor has not been in business for a long time or if the amount of time it has been franchising is not very long.

When a franchisor starts selling franchisees, the results of early franchisees are harder to predict. Even though the franchisor has been successfully operating a business for many years, there is no proven track record for how successful franchisees will be selling the same products or services.

The results from franchisees doing the same things the franchisor does may differ for many reasons. Even if the system was tested extensively before franchising, it is typical in the early years of franchising for flaws in the system to emerge. As a result, the system's methods, manuals, and tools need tweaking.

Another reason is that the franchisees do not have the same experience as the franchisor. They may also differ because of local market variations, competition, site differences, and, most of all, the franchisee's ability.

In their early years of franchising, franchisors are also more likely to be in a weaker financial position than when they have many franchisees. A younger franchise system may not have the number of units needed to generate adequate cash flow for the franchisor to support their franchisees and upgrade the system properly.

KEY POINT: When a franchisor depends on franchise fees from new unit sales, it could be more desperate to sell units to generate needed revenue.

The risk involved goes down significantly if your franchise is bought from a franchisor with a system that has been tested and refined with a proven method of operation that has succeeded in many different marketplaces. The risk goes down if the franchisor has worked out the "kinks" in the system experienced by their franchisees. As a result, unlike when starting a business from scratch, you don't have to develop the methods or things you need to operate the business successfully. You just need to apply the system and use the tools as you are supposed to. You will be provided with the things you need for your business to succeed, such as the website, marketing materials, selling methods, etc.

#2: Training and Support

Ideally, franchisors provide the training and support needed for their franchisees to succeed. This support will be significant to the success of your business.

The training provided by franchisors includes initial training of new franchisees before your franchised business is launched. This initial training prepared the franchisee to open and operate the franchised business properly.

Franchisors also provide ongoing training based on best practices and ideas drawn from their experience and knowledge of the franchisor and the system's franchisees. This may be provided through workshops, seminars, or conferences.

The support includes access to a manual for franchisees to use to operate their franchised business. The operating manual covers most things needed to run the business, from marketing to recruiting personnel to training franchisees on how to sell the products or services of the company.

Some systems have Master franchisees, and other franchisors do not. If there are Master franchisees, the Master franchisees are typically responsible for recruiting and supporting unit franchisees in their Master territories and may or not be involved in providing initial training. If the franchise you are considering involves a Master franchisee who will be the prime party for supporting you, be sure that you both feel comfortable with the Master and believe that you would enjoy working with the Master before you sign your franchise agreement.

KEY POINT: Franchising is an excellent way to be in business *for* yourself but not *by* yourself

The support franchisors provide for their franchisees typically includes proprietary technology, products, and tools that can significantly affect results. This support also includes technical assistance using the system to get the best results. The cost spent by a franchisor on creating the technology is typically much more than an individual franchisee, by itself, would be able or willing to invest in creating it.

#3: Consistently Improving System

Ideally, your chances of succeeding improve if you follow the system that is reflected in the system's operations manual. But good franchisors always look for ways to improve the system and recommend these to franchisees. This might involve new ways of doing things. It might involve adding or removing products or services that can be offered.

The improvements to the system do not come about just from the franchisor. Some of the best advancements in franchise systems come about by franchisees sharing their best practices. It's common for franchisors to further develop the suggestions from franchisees that the franchisor agrees with and then integrate them into their systems for all their franchisees to use.

When franchisors are open to their franchisees providing feedback and suggestions for improving the system, it benefits all the franchisees in the system. So, it's essential that a franchisor encourages franchisees to share their views on improving the system.

One of the ways franchisees share their views on addressing challenges and taking advantage of opportunities is during franchisor-produced franchisee conferences. Another time that this type of sharing of views occurs is during conference calls for franchisees produced by the franchisors. Also, most franchise systems have franchisee committees that provide peer advice for improving the system and the results of the franchisees in the system.

#4: Franchisee Marketing Fund

A marketing fund provides Franchisees with a marketing advantage that few "solo acts" can compete against because they can not afford the cost involved. In most franchise systems, franchisees are required to contribute a percentage of their gross revenue, or a specific amount of money, per month to a marketing fund. The greater the number of franchisees contributing to the marketing fund, the more effectively the fund can bring value to the franchisees.

Generally, decisions on how the franchisor's marketing committee money is spent will include input from selected franchisees. Examples of how marketing fund money is used include the following:

- Advertising to bring about customer/client leads and name recognition/ brand awareness
- Development and keeping up to date a professional-looking website that gives franchisees credibility with prospective customers/ clients
- Developing and testing marketing strategies, tactics, and methods
- Creating professional-looking marketing materials, media releases, and templates for such promotional materials that franchisees can use, such as brochures, emails, press releases
- Creating marketing tools for franchisees to use
- Doing marketing research to determine the demand for new marketing approaches or new products or services

#5: Greater Buying Power

Being part of a franchise system can deliver collective buying power to buy larger quantities than a non-franchisee business owner would be able to buy individually. This gives leverage to negotiate lower prices with better terms for products and supplies used by the franchisees.

#6: Name Recognition

Being part of a franchise system may provide greater name recognition for the name of a franchisee business. When there is positively viewed name recognition, there is a greater likelihood that prospective customers or clients will trust the new franchise's company. It signals that you will provide a product or service that meets the standards associated with the franchise's name. This, in turn, allows the franchise unit to compete better against established competition and start and ramp up faster to success.

CHAPTER ELEVEN- CONS OF OWNING A FRANCHISE

Now that you know about the many benefits of being a franchisee in a franchise system, it is time for some wet-blanket reality. You must consider two "cons" that might dissuade you from starting a franchise business. One con involves franchisor requirements that control how you operate your business. The other con is the funding you will need to handle the obligations of being a franchisee.

Let's look at each of the cons.

Section One: Franchisor Requirements

The underlying principle of franchising is that franchisors need some control over their franchisees' operations to ensure that the franchise business system runs effectively and uniformly. So, understand that when you buy a franchise, *you relinquish some control over operating your business.*

This control by the franchisor is done through requirements that limit the ability of franchisees to exercise their business judgment of what they can do when running their businesses and also identifies things they must do. Franchisor requirements are outlined in the franchise agreement and also in the operating manual provided by the franchisor.

The requirements differ significantly among franchise opportunities. You will have to decide if you are comfortable with the level of control the franchisor of the system you are considering will have on how you operate your business.

The following are common requirements that control how franchisees run their franchised businesses.

#1: Premises Location Requirements

If you are operating the business out of your home, there may be requirements for the setup. If you are not running the business out of your home, a franchisee may be required to purchase or lease a specific type of property to operate the franchised business.

You may need to get the franchisor's approval of the location where you will. The franchisor may even have the right to select a particular location for you to use to operate the business.

#2: Premises Look and Layout Requirements

The franchisor may also require a specific look involving a franchisor-approved uniform design for the premises and specific furniture and fixtures. The purpose of the uniform look and layout is to give customers or clients the feeling that they know what to expect when they enter the premises. A franchisee has the advantage of having a uniform look and layout because it can reduce the time needed to get the business ready to open for business.

#3: Equipment and Uniforms Requirements

Franchisors may require their franchisees to use specific equipment in operating their business. They may also require employees of the franchisees to wear specific distinctive uniforms.

#4: Marketing Requirements

Franchisees are typically required to spend a minimum amount of money within specific timelines for certain marketing types to be done by franchisees within a specific marketing area. Franchisees may be prohibited from marketing their goods or services outside a specific geographic area.

#5: Pricing Products or Services Requirements

Where it is legal to do so, franchisors often require franchisees to sell their goods or services at minimum or maximum prices. The legality of doing this is dependent on where the franchise operates.

#6: Products, Services, Supplies, and Raw Materials Requirements

Because franchisors want uniformity in the look and quality of their products and services, they may control which products and services their franchisees may sell. It is also common for franchisors to require franchisees to purchase only certain goods or services that can only be bought from suppliers approved by the franchisor.

Franchisors may require their franchisees to buy an initial amount of inventory and supplies to have in stock when they open for business and to maintain ongoing inventory minimums of certain products. Franchisees may be required to use only certain raw materials to make the products.

Franchisees may be restricted from offering new products or service lines without the franchisor's approval.

It is also common for franchisors to require franchisees to buy specific minimum quantities of supplies and raw materials and to buy the raw materials only from franchisor-approved suppliers.

#7: Employee Requirements

To operate the business franchisees may be required to employ a minimum number of specific types of employees, such as managers or staff personnel. They may also require that certain employees receive a minimum of training before starting their work activities.

Section Two: Costs

It should come as no surprise to you that there are costs that new franchisees must be prepared to handle, which they would not incur if they started their businesses from scratch. Some expenses are for upfront fees when the franchise agreement is signed. Other required payments must be incurred before the franchisee business opens or during the initial period after the franchisee opens for business. This initial period is commonly referred to as the launch period.

Let's look at some of the costs you need to be prepared to incur as a franchise, which you would not have if you started your business from scratch.

#1: Initial Franchise Fee

New franchisees must pay an initial one-time fee before signing their franchise agreement. This fee is typically called an Initial Franchise Fee. The amount of the fee varies significantly among franchise offerings. It also varies with the size of the exclusive territory the franchisee is receiving if the franchisee is getting an exclusive territory in which to operate. A smaller exclusive territory generally has a smaller initial franchise fee than a larger exclusive territory.

Another factor that impacts the fee amount is how long the franchise system has been operating. The initial franchise fee for a mature franchise system with many years of a proven track record of success by its franchisees will typically be higher than that a similar franchisor charges during the early stages of franchising.

Most franchisors require the initial Franchise Fee to be paid in full by their franchisees before they start initial training. Other franchisors permit deferred payment of some portion of the fee to be paid later.

#2: Initial Training Fees

Franchisors provide initial training for their franchisee before they begin operations. Many franchisors charge a separate initial training fee. Other franchisors do not charge an initial training fee and instead include the initial training as something received by the franchisee for paying the initial franchise fee.

#3: Ongoing Fees and Expenses

There are costs that unit franchisees are required to incur. The franchisor's disclosure document should have a section that shows not only what a franchisee needs to spend to open for business but also the projected amount needed to be spent during the initial period the business will be operating.

The following are typical ongoing fees and expenses that franchisees incur:

- **Expenses To Get The Business Ready To Open For Business In A Uniform Manner.** Costs need to be incurred to bring consistency among the system franchisees. Such expenses can include remodeling and purchasing raw materials, goods, equipment, fixtures, and uniforms. There may also be costs for the required hiring and training of employees so that they are ready when it is time to open for business.

- **Opportunity Fee or Royalty Fee.** Franchisees must pay their franchisor an opportunity or royalty fee, typically after each month of operation. The franchise agreement spells out what the franchisee gets in return for paying this ongoing fee. It usually involves such things as the franchisees being allowed to use the franchisor's system for operating the business and being allowed to use the franchisor's trade name, logo, and other commercial symbols and patents.

  If the fee is an opportunity fee, it is typically a specific amount of money that must be paid to the franchisor monthly. The amount generally escalates over time.

  If it is a royalty fee, the fee is based on a percentage of the gross sales generated from the unit franchise operations. It is also generally paid monthly. Royalty fees usually have minimum amounts of money to be paid regardless of the sales results of the franchisee. The minimums typically escalate over time. Franchises operating with exclusive territories that are in smaller territories may have minimums that are less than for those franchisees operating in large exclusive territories because they have fewer revenue opportunities.

- **Marketing Related Expenses.** It is common for franchisors to require a minimum monthly or quarterly marketing to attract clients or customers. This is in addition to payments made by franchisees to the marketing fund.

- **Advanced or Specialized Certification Training Fees.** Franchisors may require their franchisees to take advanced or specialized certification training and pay the franchisor an additional charge to take the training.

- **Administration Fees.** Franchisors may provide administrative support. An example would be collecting money for work done by franchisees. When this is provided, it is common for the franchisor to charge an administration fee.

Conclusion

When deciding whether to buy a franchise, consider whether you are willing to and would feel comfortable with following the franchisor's requirements for how you will operate your business as a franchisee. Also, consider whether you are willing and able to invest the amounts you will be required to spend as a franchisee.

If you need to arrange for financing for your business, whether a franchised business or a business started from scratch, you will find a chapter on funding later in this book. The chapter will help you identify where to go for financing and how to package your money request.

PART SIX: SELECTING THE RIGHT FRANCHISE FOR YOU

Think again if you are not exploring a franchise because you think you won't see one that matches well with your personality, background, financial position, skill set, or passion. You can find franchise opportunities in every imaginable shape, size, product, and service.

That large variety of possibilities is one reason why franchising has enabled many people to enjoy owning successful businesses. But, because there is a remarkable diversity of franchise opportunities, there are steps you need to take so that you don't waste your time checking out franchise opportunities that are not good fits for you.

CHAPTER TWELVE: SEARCHING FOR A FRANCHISE THAT IS THE BEST FIT FOR YOU

Many consider the process of selecting a franchise to be overwhelming. But it does not have to be if you follow the steps shared below.

Step One: Things to do Before you Start Your Search

Before you search for available franchise opportunities for those that seem to be a potentially good fit for you, take an honest look at yourself. To do this, consider what you have identified in your self-evaluation, including your behavioral style and your Personal Vision Statement, which you have hopefully completed following the guidelines in this book. If you have not already done them, do them now.

Then answer the following questions about yourself:

- Do you want to start a business in which you will stay involved part-time, a part-time business to blossom into a full-time involvement, or do you want to start a full-time business?
- Is there an activity you enjoy that could be part of what you want to do in a business you own?
- What is the income you want to earn from the business?

- What is the largest amount of money, including what you have and what you could borrow, that you would be comfortable investing in a business?
- Do you have any formal education or experience that you could use in a business that would help the business succeed?

Step Two: Identify Several Franchise Opportunities That Might be a Good Fit for you

Once you have the things mentioned in Step One, it is relatively easy to identify franchise opportunities that might be a good fit for you. The following are three of the most common and easiest ways to find franchise opportunities that could be a good fit for you:

#1: Use the Internet

The internet is a great way to quickly find franchise opportunities you might like to investigate further. It's fast, efficient, and costs nothing. You just put in search words such as "franchise opportunities in (country)" or "best franchise opportunities in (country)." You can even narrow things down in your research based on the amount you can invest with search words such as "top franchisees under $50,000."

#2: Attend Franchisor Shows

Attending franchise expositions is a great way to meet with representatives of franchisors who will share information about their franchise opportunities. They will not have the time at the show to discuss their franchise opportunities in detail. But you should have time to get answers to your questions that will help you understand their opportunity better. For example, you will know if the opportunity is within your investment limitations.

You will receive information that will help you compare different offerings and know which franchise opportunities you want to learn more about. You may decide to schedule a time with the representative to have a follow-up meeting later after the show.

While at the franchisors' booths, the franchisor's representatives will give you promotional literature that you can review later.

#3: Use a Franchise Broker

Franchise brokers represent many franchise opportunities that the brokers can discuss with you. Some brokers operate alone, and others are associated with broker organizations. They can be found by searching on the internet for franchise brokers in your country. Franchise brokers sometimes refer to themselves as franchise consultants or coaches instead of being referred to as franchise brokers.

Some franchise brokers charge you nothing upfront to work with you. Others charge upfront fees, but generally not large amounts upfront because franchise brokers get paid a large commission if you *buy a franchise presented to you by the broker*.

Before a franchise broker suggests franchise opportunities for you to consider, the broker will ask you questions and may ask you to fill out a questionnaire. After analyzing your answers and questionnaire information, the broker will suggest several franchisor opportunities you should consider.

If you decide to use a broker, interview a few brokers to evaluate their professionalism and your comfort level with them before selecting which franchise broker to use.

RED FLAG WARNING: Be aware that some brokers might push you toward franchisees that offer them the highest commissions. But good brokers will show you what they think is best for you even if the franchisor is not offering them the largest commission.

Step Three: Go to Franchisors' Websites

Regardless of how you find out about franchise opportunities that could interest you, get more information about the franchise opportunities by visiting the franchisors' websites. Their websites will provide you with an overview of their franchise offerings. Many franchisors share profiles on the websites of their ideal franchisee prospect.

It may include information about the experience or skill set they want their franchisees to have. For example, TAB's website explains that TAB requires its new franchisee prospects to have C-level executive, business owner, or executive coach experience.

If you are interested in knowing more about a franchise opportunity after reviewing a website, go back to the website and check the franchisor's website more carefully to come up with questions you can ask when meeting later with a franchisor's sales representative.

Then send an email to the franchisor, following the instructions on the website, expressing your interest in knowing more about the franchise offering. You will be contacted by someone handling franchise sales for the franchisor. The sales specialist will try to schedule time with you for a telephone or virtual meeting.

In addition, you will usually receive such things as a virtual brochure about the franchise offering and a link to one or more videos that will inform you of some basic things about the franchise opportunity.

Once you have this information, you should be able to narrow down the list of franchise opportunities that interest you to no more than several options.

Step Four: Meetings with Franchisor Sales Representative

Your meetings with franchisor sales representatives take place by phone or virtually. You will get a lot of information, but be aware that the franchisor representative may not be able to answer some of your answers because of laws prohibiting giving specific information to franchisee prospects. The representative will tell you that the answer can not legally be given to you in this situation.

Your First Meeting

Your first meeting with a franchisor representative will typically include the representative explaining the franchisor's process for moving a new franchisee prospect from the first meeting you are having to the endpoint of signing a franchise agreement. At this meeting, you will typically be able to ask a limited number of questions. These questions fall into one of the following three categories:

List One Questions: These questions are questions specific to the particular franchise opportunity that you created from looking at the franchisor's website

List Two Questions: These questions involve anything in the offering that you consider essential and feel that you do not understand, such as the length of the franchise's initial term, renewal rights, or rights to sell or assign the franchise agreement

List Three Questions: This is a short list of questions you must ask all franchise sales representatives with whom you are having meetings if the franchisor's representative has not shared the information during the meeting. This short list should include such things as the following questions:

- Does the franchisor have a location available for you in an area where you would like to operate a business? If the answer is no, you might not want to spend more time investigating the particular franchise opportunity. Not surprisingly, you will find that a newer system is more likely to be able to offer you prime territories that you like compared to a mature system that has already sold many of the best territories to its current franchisees.

- How much and how often will you have to pay into the marketing fund? How will the marketing funds be used, and what input do franchisees have on how the money is used?

- Has a former franchisee failed in the general area where you are considering operating the franchise, and if so, what is the contact information of that former franchisee? You will want to contact that former franchisee to get the person's views on why the franchise failed.

- Does the franchisor have the right to terminate a franchise agreement early, and if so, what would give the franchisor the right to terminate the franchise agreement early?

- Does the franchisee have the right to terminate the franchise agreement early? If so, what is the financial penalty for doing so?

- Are there restrictions on franchisees after the termination of their franchise agreements?

Your Second Meeting and Other Follow-Up Meetings

Your second and third meetings with franchisor sales representatives often include a slide-type presentation about the opportunity, with time allocated for your questions.

By the time you have completed your second or third meeting, it's essential that you have a good handle on some crucial non-financial and also financial things in the franchise offerings, such as the following:

#1 Non-Financial Factors: The important non-financial factors you need to know at this point are such things as:

- How long has the franchisor been operating? And how long has the franchisor been franchising?
- Length of the Initial Term
- Renewal rights to extend the agreement with one renewal or a series of renewals under certain conditions for exercising the renewal rights
- Franchisor rights to terminate a franchise agreement early for a cause, such as the failure of the franchisee to achieve minimum performance levels or the loss of the lease for the premises in which the franchisee operates
- Restrictions on a franchisee's rights to sell or assign the franchise agreement without the franchisor's approval or whether franchisees have to offer to sell their franchises first back to the franchisor
- The franchise includes an exclusive or protected territory prohibiting the franchisors are prohibited from selling one of their franchises to anyone else in that territory. An exclusive territory helps a franchisee selling the franchised unit to get a higher price for the sale.

#2 Financial Factors: The investment needed for all related financial commitments you would be taking on if you bought the franchise for things as:

- The amount of their franchise fees and whether they have to be paid in a lump sum or can be paid out in installments. A newer franchise system is more likely to offer a lower franchise fee and give pay-out terms for the franchise fee versus more established ones. This is probably because the risk of failure with a newer franchise system is higher.

- The amount of the initial training fees, if not included in the franchise fees, how many days of initial training are provided by the franchisor, and if initial training is provided in-person, virtual, or a combination of both. The latter point is important since you will have travel and accommodation costs if the initial training is in person.

- The cost of additional training and support provided by the franchisors after initial training for you and your employees who receive training

- The cost of the franchisor sending a mentor-type person to your place of business for "pre-launch and launch" support before you open for business and during the early days after your opening for business

- The amount of opportunity or royalty fees, including any minimum amounts that you must pay

- The amount, if any, of purchases you are required to make from the franchisors for products or supplies

- The fees to attend franchisor-produced conferences for franchisees
- The costs, if any, of using the franchisors' proprietary technology
- Any charge for the administrative services provided by the franchisors, such as providing billing of customers or clients
- Other working capital

Step Five: Narrow Your List Down to Three Franchise Opportunities

After you have had your second or third meetings with the sales representative of several different franchise opportunities, it's time to narrow down your list to no more than your top three franchise opportunities with which you will be investigating deeper. When narrowing down the list, you will consider the answers to the questions above. But in addition, consider such things as:

- Will you be able to use your experience and skills in the business?
- Does the opportunity fit with your personal vision of what you would like your future to be?
- Does the business project an image that associates with a type of image you want, such as being a professional advisor?

- Are you okay with the financial terms, including the franchise fee and all other investments required?

Some take the additional step of asking their bankers to order a credit report for the franchisor. They don't want to include a franchisor with credit problems on their shortlist.

When you have narrowed the list to no more than three franchise opportunities, it is time for you to dive deep into those franchise offerings on the shortlist. This deep dive begins with you asking those franchisors on the list for copies of their disclosure documents.

If you live in a country where disclosure documents are not required, it is up to you to ask the franchisor for a disclosure document. Make it clear to the franchisor that you won't move ahead without a franchise disclosure document, including their franchise agreements.

Step Six: Review Disclosure Documents and Franchise Agreements

You should be able to rely on information in the disclosure documents you receive from the franchisors because misrepresentations subject them to civil and even criminal penalties. The following are among the things you need to review in the disclosure documents, which are essential for you to look for so that you can make an informed decision on which franchise to buy:

- Earnings claims by franchisors about the average gross revenue earnings generated by current franchisees or the average of the top percentage of their franchisees. Some franchisors even include earnings claims for their company-owned outlets. NOTE: In many countries, franchisors are not required to make earnings claims. If no earnings claim is provided, your alternative for finding out the information is to ask current franchisees about their earnings when you conduct your validation calls.

- The financial statements for each of the franchisor's most recent years. The financial strength/health of the franchisors is essential because a financially strong franchisor is likelier to provide a high level of support services and is more likely to be around for many years in the future. If you are not comfortable reviewing the financial statements for such things as the amount of equity, net profits, cash position, and current assets to current liabilities ratios, you may want to get help doing so from a professional.

- List of names and locations of current franchisees and former franchisees in the franchise systems that you might select to contact for validation calls

- Material litigation involving a franchisor with a history of the franchisors suing franchisees or franchisees suing the franchisors
- Any bankruptcy filed by the franchisors
- Any felony conviction of the franchisor or issuance of an injunction against the franchisor, particularly one relating to a violation of franchise law
- Information about the executives, including their experience, how long they have been employed, and whether they have been involved in a bankruptcy, engaged in any material litigation, or convicted of a felony
- The number of franchisees that have left the franchise system in recent years

Concerns or Need Further Explanations After Reading Disclosure Documents

If you have concerns or need further explanations after reading the disclosure document but are still interested in the franchise, meet with the franchisor's sales representative to discuss your concerns. The following are a few common examples of concerns by prospects after reading disclosure documents.

#1. If litigation involving a franchisor concerns you, mainly if it involves franchisees suing the franchisors claiming they did not live up to the terms of the franchise agreements, ask for information about the litigation. Knowing if the franchisors were held liable or settled the cases is important.

#2. If the number of franchisees who have left the system seems high, this could be a sign of a problem with the system. The franchisor's representative may or may not provide good reasons for the situation that satisfies you.

#3. If you have concerns about whether the company is financially sound.

If you don't get answers that remove your concerns, you might want to walk or run away from that franchise opportunity.

KEY POINT: If a franchisor has made critical promises to you, not in the franchisor's disclosure document, get the promises in writing and ensure that the franchisor signs them.

Step Seven: Schedule Discovery Visits with the Finalist Franchisors

What you learn during and after your Discovery visits will help you narrow your short list of franchise opportunities to the one you want to pursue that best fits you. So, after you have carefully read the disclosure document and have no concerns, or if your concerns have been alleviated after a meeting with the franchisor's representative to discuss them, it's time for you to schedule Discovery visits with those franchisors that still interest you.

Some franchisors will offer only virtual Discovery visits, some only in-person visits, and some will give you the option of whether you want to make Discovery virtually or in person. In-person visits are typically only one day, and some franchisors will pay part of the travel and accommodation expenses you incur to attend the Discovery visit. Virtual Discoveries are often spread over two days, so prospects don't have to spend too many hours on the computer during any given day.

Before Discovery Visit

Different franchisors look for other things in evaluating whether a prospect is someone they would want as a franchisee. So, after scheduling your Discovery visit and before it starts, it's common for the franchisor to require franchisee prospects to complete an application that shows personal history, fill out a questionnaire or survey, sign a confidentiality agreement and provide certain financial information.

The application will ask you to identify your management and other job experience. This is important to the franchisor because some franchise opportunities require a minimum number of years of management experience or type of executive experience. For example, TAB has turned down franchisee candidates who did not have C-level experience nor were former business owners.

The questionnaire or survey helps the franchisors understand things about you, including attributes you might bring to the franchise business. Some franchisors will ask you to complete behavioral surveys to understand you better.

The franchisors will typically require you to sign a confidentiality agreement to confirm that you will not disclose any information you receive to any third party other than your professional advisors (lawyer, accountant, bank manager, for example).

They will also request financial data that typically. The information includes your current income, assets, debts, and whether you have ever been bankrupt. Franchisors use this to judge whether a prospect might be under-capitalized or the indebtedness of the candidate is too high.

Step Eight: Validation with Current and Former Franchisees

After you've scheduled your Discovery visits, reach out to current and former franchisees of the franchisor to schedule time for so-called "validation calls." You can find their addresses and contact information in the disclosure document you receive from the franchisor.

If the laws where you live do not require the franchisor to share this information with you, let the franchisor know that you need the information before you can move ahead.

Select the existing and former franchisees you want to reach out to for validation calls, starting with those who operate in markets similar to where you are considering. When you talk to them, please show respect that they are not getting paid for their time talking with you and are running businesses.

Manage your expectations. Some on your list will not want to take time out to take your validation calls. Some you talk with will not be open with you. Also, when you do have a validation call, you may not be able to get through your complete list of questions.

If someone tells you that they have had problems with the franchisor, ask them to be as specific about the issues as they feel comfortable sharing with you. Don't assume that the franchisee is being fair when blaming the franchisor. The reality might be that the franchisee is not following the franchisor's recommended system the way the franchisee is supposed to follow it.

Be prepared with your list of questions before you speak with the current or former franchisees so that you don't waste their time. This will help you keep the conversations as "tight" as possible.

Validation Calls with Current Franchisees

The following are questions you should consider having in the list you use for validation calls with current franchisees:

- Do you view your franchise business as successful?
- Would you be comfortable sharing with me the gross revenue for your business last year?
- If your business is profitable, how long did it take until it became profitable?
- Does the franchisor have controls on your business that make it hard for you to operate?
- What did you do workwise before buying the franchise?
- Did the franchisor mislead you about significant expenses or investments you had to make to start your business or during the early stage after you started?
- Do you feel that the franchisor has lived up to your commitments, such as providing training, training materials, and support at a professional level?
- Would you buy the franchise if you had to do it over again?
- Are the franchisor's employees competent with a good attitude about working with you?

- How would you rate the franchisor's Operations Manual, including the marketing and sales methodology and tools?

Validation Calls with Former Franchisees

When you make validation calls with former franchisees, one of the questions you ask them should be, "Why did you leave the franchise system?" If the answer is that the business failed, ask, "Why do you think the business failed?" Keep in mind that the failure could be that the former franchisee didn't follow the system, and you will not likely hear that as a response. The franchisor might have even terminated the former franchisee.

The reason you hear for leaving the franchise system might not involve a system failure. The following are three of the most common examples of this:

- They sold their businesses
- They faced unexpected challenges outside the control of franchisors, like the pandemic the world experienced starting in 2020
- The term of their franchise agreements expired, and they didn't renew the agreement

You may hear things during the validation calls you want to bring up during your Discovery visit with the franchisor.

Step Nine: Your Discovery Visits

It would be best if you did not decide whether to become a franchisee of a franchise system until you have your Discovery visit with the franchisor. While you evaluate the franchisor and the franchisor's team, they will evaluate you.

During your Discovery visit, you will attend sessions where you will experience presentations from different members of the franchisor team. This usually starts with an introduction session in which, among other things, the franchisor will describe the company's vision for the future.

This introduction session is generally followed by sessions for each key area that impacts the franchise's operations. For example, one of the sessions typically focuses on understanding the quality of initial and ongoing training and support as well as the support the franchisor provides.

Find out who will be the experienced and qualified mentor provided by the franchisor to help you launch your business. You also want to be shown how to access the franchisor's best practices so that you can determine if it's user-friendly.

Each session is typically conducted by key franchisor team members, such as department heads. An example of this would be the session on marketing being handled by the franchisor's marketing director.

In some ways, the interaction during a Discovery visit is like a job interview. For example, during the sessions, the franchisor's team members will typically ask questions about yourself, your motivation for buying a franchise, and relevant work experience.

The presenters of the sessions will share their evaluation of you with the selection committee of the franchisor. Those delivering the sessions will judge you, such as whether they feel they can work with you or think you could be a "problem franchisee." They will evaluate how well you communicate and how committed you seem to be about doing what it takes to succeed as a franchisee. They may decide that you are not qualified or will not follow the franchisor's guidelines and system.

You will also be evaluated on the questions you ask. Franchisors expect you to ask them questions during your Discovery visit, and be concerned if you don't ask any questions. They will size up the quality of the questions you ask, so before starting your Discovery visit, you need to create a list of questions you will ask. The following are examples of the common questions that prospects ask during Discovery visits:

- Who will be the person supporting me, and how often will the person's communications occur?
- Who will be the trainers who do the initial training, and what are their qualifications?

- Can I see a demonstration of the proprietary technology your franchisees are required to use so that I better understand its value and user-friendliness?

Also, be prepared to bring up anything you have heard during your validation calls at the Discovery visit that concern you. But do not tell the franchisor the name of the current or former franchisee who told you about the problem. The franchisor may provide information that will help you to overcome your concerns. If your concerns are still strong after your Discovery visit, it might be time to move away from that franchise opportunity.

KEY POINT: During your Discovery visit, you will get to know the franchisor's team members with whom you will work if you buy a franchise.

Step Ten: Franchisors Post Discovery Selection Process

After you have completed your Discovery visits, you should know which of the offerings is your first choice for the one you want to buy. Of course, there's always the possibility that the selection committee of the franchisor will decide that you will not be offered the opportunity to become a franchisee with the franchisor.

Let the sales specialist of the selected franchise system know that you want to move ahead. You will receive the franchisor's application form, which will ask for a lot of information about you, such as previous jobs, personal and business referees, and some detailed financial information.

Step Eleven: Engage an Attorney with Franchise Experience to Review the Franchise Agreement Before Signing it

Before engaging an attorney to review the franchise agreement, you might want to do additional research on the internet. Check whether non-litigation complaints have been filed against the franchisor by any of its customers or clients relating to its services, products, or personnel by any consumer protection agencies. If there have been non-litigation complaints filed against the franchisor, you might want to ask the franchisor for an explanation of the situation. If you don't like the answer of the franchisor, you might stop your interest in becoming a franchisee.

The franchise agreement will govern the legal relationship between you and the franchisor for the term of the franchise agreement. So, before signing a franchise agreement, engage an attorney experienced in franchise law. An experienced franchise attorney should know what to look for when reviewing the disclosure document, including the franchise agreement.

After reviewing the document, the attorney will discuss anything in the franchisor's disclosure document, including the franchise agreement, that should or might concern you. This includes any obligations you will be responsible for executing under the franchise agreement as a franchisee.

The attorney will typically recommend that you form a legal entity that would become the franchise owner instead of you to create another barrier against personal liability.

The attorney will point out things in the franchise agreement that the attorney recommends for you to try to negotiate and make sure you understand binding legal obligations such as, but not limited to:

- Whether you can legally cancel the franchise agreement after you have signed it within a time called the "cooling-off" period and, if so, how many days are in the cooling-off period
- Your rights as a franchisee to sell the franchise and, if you can, under what conditions
- What is covered by the personal guarantee the franchisor is asking you to give
- What type of protection the franchisor's name and trademark would give your business legally, along with potential trademark problems the attorney sees that could affect your business

- Restrictions on the goods or services you can sell or against your right to expand the business to a larger location or marketing to a larger area
- Restrictions against your being able to relocate your business
- Requirements giving the franchisor pre-approval for the location you pick as to where you want to operate or for any design or signs
- Rights of the franchisors require you to make periodic renovations
- Franchisor controls how you conduct your business, such as you having to be open during certain hours
- Requirements that you purchase products or supplies only from approved suppliers or from the franchisor
- Whether there is a specific number of days before you can sign the franchise agreement, you must have the disclosure document, and the franchise agreement, for the signed franchise agreement to be effective
- Conditions that would legally allow the franchisor to terminate your franchise agreement before your agreement expiration date

KEY POINT: An experienced franchise attorney will not need to learn about franchise law, reducing the hours you will have to pay the attorney.

Step Twelve: Execute the Franchise Agreement

When you are ready to buy the franchise, ask the franchisor to provide you with copies of the franchise agreement to sign. Most franchisee prospects want to negotiate terms in the franchise agreement. However, keep in mind that there could be a problem for the franchisor if the franchisor makes a material change to the terms for you not in the franchise agreement registered with the proper government bodies or agencies.

Suppose such a material change is given to you in your franchise agreement. In that case, the franchisor may legally be required to file an added registration that acknowledges the particular terms you give. As a result, many things in the franchise agreement are non-negotiable if the franchise agreement has been filed and approved by a governmental body.

Conclusion

I hope you realize that selecting the best franchise for you does not have to be overwhelming. All you need to do is focus on each of the steps shared with you in this chapter before going to the next step.

One of the advantages of buying a franchise is that you will benefit from the experience of other franchisees and the franchisor. You will receive information, training, and support for everything you need to know to get your new business ready to open its doors for business and then run the business successfully.

KEY POINT: If you are considering buying a retail store franchise, you may want to spend a few hours visiting the retail stores of one or more parties with whom you did validation calls to help evaluate whether you would enjoy being the owner/operator of such a franchise.

PART SEVEN: THINGS TO DO BEFORE BUSINESS OPENS WHEN STARTING A BUSINESS FROM SCRATCH

Whether you buy a franchise or start a business from scratch, you probably want to start your business because you don't want to work for someone else. You want to be your own boss instead of an employee. But the question is should you start a business by buying a franchise or start your business from scratch?

Buying a franchise is not for everyone. For many, starting businesses from scratch is a better fit. They would not enjoy being part of a franchise system even if they have the financial ability to handle the upfront investment and ongoing required cost needed to own and operate a franchise.

So when deciding on a franchise versus from scratch, take an honest look at yourself. For example, if you have the nature of a maverick constantly looking for ways to change things and innovate, it may be best for you to consider starting your business from scratch.

Will you be okay with the franchisor controlling how you run your business and the changes you want to make to the business? When you are part of a franchise system, you may suggest improvements to the system because you believe you have a better way of doing things. However, the

197

improvements you recommend may not find their way into the basic system you are to follow because the franchisor controls that decision.

If you don't like conforming to someone else's system and feel this level of control over how you run your business and what products or services your business can sell are unacceptable, you probably would not like to be a franchisee.

Also, if you dream of building your business into a much larger company and want control over the expansion, this dream would not fit with most franchise opportunities.

There is another big positive to starting your business from scratch. It takes place when the business succeeds because it will bring you greater fulfillment knowing that the success came from your building the business rather than the success coming about because you used a system created by someone else.

KEY POINT: Don't be under the impression that building a business from scratch will be easy. Because, to the contrary, it is challenging. You would need to do and create many things that would be provided to you if your business were part of a franchise system.

CHAPTER THIRTEEN: YOU

Introduction

When you start a business from scratch, It's no exaggeration when I say that **you** are the key. **You** are the driver of your business. There is no franchisor telling you how and when to do things and providing things you need to use to succeed. So, it's up to **you** to make things happen.

Do you see a theme here? Yes, **you** will need to do many things before your new start-from-scratch business opens its doors for business. For your business to succeed, **you** will need such things as:

- A founder mindset
- Clarity on **your** role in your business
- **Your** long-term vision for the business

Founder Mindset

Ideas are just dreams without actions. Many people have wanted to start businesses from scratch and had great ideas for the businesses. But they never launched their businesses. One of the most common reasons for this is that they were overwhelmed with what had to be done.

When you start your business from scratch, you need a founder's mindset. This mindset embraces the reality that it will take hard work, time, and decisions about how your business will do things. You will often experience that you "did not know what you don't know."

You need to be mentally prepared to handle the emotional turmoil most entrepreneurs face when starting a business from ground zero. This is particularly true during the pre-opening period and the early years of the business.

If you are like most founders, you will also have to be mentally prepared to make an income sacrifice during the early years of the business. It typically takes up to two years for most started-from-scratch businesses to provide an income to their founders that gets them back to, or above, the earnings level they had before starting their businesses.

Your Role in the Business

It's up to you to define what your role will be. You are in charge, but what will you do in the business? It would be best to decide how best to use your energies and time in your business. Your role should take advantage of your areas of strength.

Do you have experience in a particular area that can help your new business succeed? If the business requires you to have specific expertise that you don't have, can you get the expertise within a reasonable time and at an affordable expense?

One SBF dreamed of starting a bakery business but had no experience working in a bakery. So, before he began the business, he took a job working in a bakery. He told me his very successful business would probably have failed if not for what he learned working for another bakery company.

Write your job description. Include what you will be doing and how much time you want to devote to the business's "big picture" strategic level matters rather than the day-to-day activities.

Vision Statement

Shortly after you decide that you want to start a particular type of business,

Write a vision statement for what you want your business to be like five to ten years in the future. I am not suggesting you write a manuscript for your long-term Vision Statement. On the contrary, it should be 100 words or less.

You might, at this point, be questioning why you need the long-term vision so early. The answer is that it is necessary to guide you and your first employees on many things needed before your business opens for business. Your written vision statement will help bring focus on and prioritization for many activities that need to be done

The following is the written TAB Vision Statement I created for TAB before TAB started:

TAB Vision Statement

- To empower TAB members to reach their long-term business visions, including greater business success and increased valuations of their businesses, and their personal visions

- To be the most respected international provider to business owners of peer advisory and coaching services

- To provide outstanding strategic planning services for privately owned businesses

- To provide real-world management development training and executive coaching services

- To provide interconnectedness for the worldwide TAB community so they can share input with others in the community

- To consistently adapt, innovate, and improve the TAB system, utilizing input from the TAB community and cutting-edge technology

I am proud that the things in my vision statement have taken place.

Share Your Company Vision Statement

Share your Company Vision Statement with the employees you hire. Doing so will help you and your employees identify your business's goals to achieve your long-term vision.

KEY POINT: Don't view sharing your long-term vision with employees as a one-time and done thing to do. Periodically ask your employees questions about the vision statement to be sure they understand it and have not lost sight of your vision.

Conclusion

By now you know if you want to start your business from scratch. You know what a founder's mindset is and what you need to do to get and maintain the type of mindset founders need to lead their businesses successfully. You will identify the role you should fulfill in your business and your long-term vision for your business.

CHAPTER FOURTEEN: PRE-OPENING STRATEGIC PLANNING

Businesses starting from scratch need good strategic plans to follow before opening. As the company's founder, it's up to you to develop up to five pre-opening strategic plans that will lead to the business launching well. Your pre-opening strategic goals will help you decide on what you need to do and stay aware of the tasks you need to complete pre-opening.

Each pre-opening strategic plan needs a goal, strategies, and action plans. The goals lead to achieving your long-term vision for your business. Determining a goal for each pre-opening strategic plan is usually straightforward, but it's not enough.

You need strategies that are conceptual to achieve each of the goals. You then need to identify SMART action plans to implement the strategies. SMART refers to the action plan being Specific, Measurable, Attainable, Relevant, and Time-Bound. The action plans are very specific but not complex. Action plans that are too complex are more likely to fail because those responsible for making the action plans work may view the plans as overwhelming.

KEY POINT: Without pre-opening strategic plans, new businesses with good ideas, products, and services have failed, which could have succeeded if their founders had created and implemented pre-opening strategic plans.

Pre-Opening Strategic Plans to Consider

When I started TAB, I identified five areas I needed to handle before TAB began operating, and I developed pre-opening strategic plans for each area. The areas are:

- Legal
- Location
- Operations
- Marketing
- Employees

KEY POINT: Don't view your pre-opening Strategic Plans as etched in stone. Instead, accept that they will need to evolve as your business gets closer to opening for business due to what you are experiencing.

The strategic plans I developed were, of course, focused on what was needed for TAB. Your strategic plans will be tailored to your business. Below I will share information for you to consider when creating the strategic pre-opening plans for your business.

Strategic Plan #1: Legal

There are legal-related things that need to be done as soon as possible:

Company Name

You need a business name. The name selection for your business needs to be done long before you open for business. Because of the legal cost of creating and registering a logo and trademark, many start-ups wait a while before engaging parties to develop logos and trademarks and then hiring attorneys to apply for trademark registrations.

So, let's focus first on the company name. What's in a company name, trademark, and logo? It could be a lot! So, take the time needed before deciding on the company's name you will use.

There are different philosophies about how to create a company name. Some choose a business name to convey a particular image. Some choose names that are easy to remember. Some business names describe something about the company's nature. Others choose names that describe the nature of the business or convey a particularly positive message or concept.

For example, I decided that TAB would operate under the name "The Alternative Board (TAB)" to convey that TAB is an alternative to a high-paid board of directors.

KEY POINT: If you are unsure of a name to use, consider asking some people you respect for their business marketing insight to tell you which name they like best for your new business.

After selecting your first choice for the name of your new business, you can search the internet for businesses using the same name or a name very similar to the one you want to use or a business in the general business field as the one you are opening. Your internet search will not show you if someone has registered the name but isn't promoting it yet still has the right to the name.

But, if things look okay for using the name after your internet search, do another search on the internet for the website of the appropriate government agency responsible for reserving names. Contact that agency to see if the name is available.

So, if you are still interested in the name after your searches, register the name through the internet with your appropriate governmental agency. Or, you can engage legal counsel to verify that the name is available and fill out the application needed to register the name.

Also, be aware that it's common for businesses to be incorporated under one name but to do business under a different name. For example, TAB is incorporated under the name TAB Boards International, Inc. But it does business as The Alternative Board or TAB.

KEY POINT: Check to see if, in your country, a business can operate under a different name from the name registered name, such as a "doing business as" or "DBA" name.

Logo and Trademark

Most businesses do not have a logo or trademark when they open for business because of the money needed to develop them and apply for trademark registration. However, you may want a logo or trademark before you open for business because you think they can help potential customers and clients remember your company's image and distinguish your company's products or services from others. If this is the case, you will need to engage someone to create them and hire a trademark attorney to register your trademark to get it legally protected.

Business Legal Structure

There are different business legal structures under which your business can operate, and each has other legal consequences. For example, the type of legal entity you use for your new business can determine such things as:

- Your personal liability exposure
- Whether income from the business can be sheltered with delayed taxes until the income is distributed
- Whether there is a fiscal year-end for the business rather than a calendar year-end for tax purposes

So, before selecting the type of legal entity, discuss with your accountant or legal advisor the legal structure alternatives and the pros and cons of each. After deciding on the kind of entity, the required filing must be done to bring your new business legally into existence.

Strategic Plan #2: Location

If you are not going to be operating your business out of your home, you need a place of business where you will operate. Unless you have a lot of experience buying or leasing commercial properties, you should engage an experienced commercial real estate agent to help you buy or lease your location. A professional commercial real estate agent should be able to show you the best locations that are zoned for your purposes and within your budget.

Before you Meet with Commercial Real Estate Agents

Before you meet with commercial real estate agents you are considering using, identify the following three things:

- Amount of Rent. What can you afford to pay in monthly mortgage payments or rent? The amount you budget for monthly mortgage payments or rent dramatically affects the type of locations available to you.

- Amount of Space You Will Need. How much space will your new business need when your business starts operating? Most start-ups lease space that allows them to grow in the initial lease term because they don't know how much space they will need in a few years. If you can afford it, the location for your business should have enough room for you to expand your business in the early years.

- Whether You Are Going to Rent or Buy the Premises You Will Be Using. Most start-ups will lease their first locations even if they have the money to buy their business location because they don't know the amount of space their businesses may require down the road if they become successful. Also, leasing helps the businesses' cash flow because less money is up compared to what would be needed if the property were purchased.

Meetings with Commercial Real Estate Agents

Meet a few commercial real estate agents before deciding who to use. Before you meet with the commercial real estate agents, be prepared to let them know some things as the importance of:

- Having a lot of visibility and walk-in traffic
- Being located within a particular driving distance for prospective customers or clients to come to your premises
- A minimum traffic count, if any, that you might want to have driven by the location
- Your customer or client prospects to easily be able to get to your business with convenient and sufficient parking
- Being in a building or area with a particular type of business mix and not another kind. For example, a law firm might want to be in a building with accountants' offices, not adult sex shops.
- The type and size of signage for your business
- Being close to a particular supplier of materials and supplies, a shipping facility, or a railroad track spur. For example, the availability of a railroad track spur was essential to why my father and uncle bought a particular property for their pillow manufacturing business. The spur cut down the delivery cost of heavy loads of feathers.

KEY POINT: Ask for a listing agreement that includes the commission paid to the agent from the seller or lessor when the lease or sale is consummated.

Terms to Negotiate

The following are some terms you should try to negotiate in the purchase agreement or lease :

- The price used for buying or leasing the property
- Special terms if buying a property, such as a payout method for paying off the purchase price
- Special terms if leasing a property such as the following:
- A free rent period
- Rent based on a percentage of your sales generated during the beginning start-up period
- Shorter initial term with more renewal periods of the lease
- Tax and common-area payment "caps" in the lease so they are not open-ended
- Leasehold improvements the lessor will make
- Fixture allowance from the leasor
- Early termination rights to get out of a lease, with only a minor penalty

- Elimination of any personal guarantee or, if not possible, a maximum cap limitation on the personal guarantee

Strategic Plan #3: Operations

You need a plan for getting the equipment, vehicles, inventory, and technology you need to have before you open for business.

Equipment

Some of the things to consider for your equipment needs include the following:

- Who will you get the equipment from, and under what terms?
- Will you be leasing the equipment or buying the equipment? For most start-up businesses, it is better to lease rather than purchase equipment. This is because you can usually put down very little money, which increases the cash available for your new company to use for other purposes.

Vehicles

What vehicles will your business need to operate? As with equipment, it is generally better for most start-up businesses to lease rather than buy vehicles because this approach will result in more money being in the business available to run the business.

Inventory

Who do you intend to buy your inventory from, and what do you need to do to get the best possible pricing and terms? Some inventory suppliers will give start-up businesses special dating terms on display merchandise and opening start-up inventory. Some will even provide their inventory or materials on consignment, which means you won't have to pay for stock *until you sell it*. (Great, right?)

In some types of businesses, you can buy your inventory at lower prices if you join a buying group. This is because the buying group has the collective purchases of its members to use as buying power to get lower prices for its buying group members. Many buying groups also develop marketing materials for the use of their members that is of a high quality that the individual members would find too expensive to develop independently.

Buying groups typically charge their members a monthly or annual fee, but the savings through lower purchase prices should greatly outway the membership fees.

Technology

You need to decide what technology your business will need to operate and your budget for the technology. Then you can determine from whom you will buy or lease the equipment.

Target Day for Grand Opening

Your target day for when you will open your business should be at a time when you have completed everything you need to accomplish before the Grand Opening. In setting the target opening date, be sure to allocate enough time to do what is required before your Grand Opening. You don't want to open your business until you are ready.

KEY POINT: Don't schedule the date for your Grand Opening until you are confident you will be ready to open on that date.

Strategic Plan #4: Marketing

You need a strategic pre-opening plan addressing how you will market your products or services. Below are some things to consider when creating your plan:

Profile of Your Potential Customers/Clients

What is the profile of your potential customers/clients? The profile includes such demographics as age, gender, location, and income level. Your marketing efforts will fail if you don't have clarity on the identity of your potential customers/clients most likely to buy from you.

In developing the profile of prospective customers or clients, research whom others in your business field are selling the same products or services.

Once you are clear as to who is your prospect targets, you need to identify how you can get contact information for targeted customers or clients. You can use many different resources to buy contact lists of your potential customers or clients so that you can direct your marketing to those who fit the profile of your potential customers or clients.

In developing the profile of your customer or client, consider such things as:

- Range of income
- Age range
- Geographic area

Your Products or Services

Trust me on this. You do not want to be the founder of a business convinced there was a market for their product or service and learn that a sufficient market did not exist. So, do what you can to determine whether there will be a demand for your product or service.

If you have decided to open a particular type of business, you must already believe that there either is an existing demand for the product or service you will sell or, if there is not, that you can create the need. But recognize that many others have started businesses feeling the same confidence about demand, and their businesses failed. Why? Because the market for the product or service offered by those start-up businesses was insufficient.

Demand for Your Products or Services

So, here's your question: How do you confirm that enough demand exists for the product or service your business will be offering to sell? You need to know this before spending your time and money to start a new business.

If there is competition in your area selling the same or similar products or services that your new business will offer, consider whether you can compete against established companies with high name recognition even if you offer the same goods and services at lower prices.

Creating demand may require you to convince prospects that there is a clear differentiation between your products or services and products and services offered by companies already established in the market. So, to compete against the established competition, look for your competitive edge. For example, do you have a cost advantage in producing your product or a unique background in providing your service?

If it seems that it is not working well for other companies offering the same products or services, try to find out why they are having trouble selling them. You might be able to learn something from their failures in selling the products or services.

KEY POINT: *Do not underestimate your competition!*

Suppose no competition in your area sells the same or similar products or services that your new business will offer. In that case, it's not necessarily good because it may indicate *no market for your product or service.* Or, it could be because no one else has the unique product or service you want to sell.

KEY POINT: It's harder, but not impossible, to determine if there is enough demand for a unique product or service you intend for your new company to sell.

To determine if there is a demand for your new product or service, you might want to conduct a "low budget" marketing survey. To do so, do the following:

- Identify the questions you want to ask to determine whether prospects want what you will offer. Among your questions will be one or more to find out if those being surveyed will pay what you need to be paid for your products or services.
- Decide if the survey will be done by sending out questionnaires or by engaging prospective customers or clients in short phone interview conversations
- Purchase a contact list of those with the profile you want to sell your products or services to and send them the survey.

When looking at demand, be careful that the need for your product or service is not because of a short-term trend that will likely turn out to be a fad.

Website

Identify what you want your website to accomplish and what you can afford to pay before engaging someone to create it. Then you, your employee, or someone you engage, need to write the copy for the website that communicates the messaging you want to convey.

When this is done, you need someone to create the website with the look and functionality that you want it to have. It would be best if you also assigned someone who will be responsible for maintaining the website and keeping it up to date with posts.

Brochure

A company brochure is a valuable marketing tool. Most new businesses have a business brochure ready to give out before opening for business. Very inexpensive software available today will allow you, or one of your employees, to create your initial brochure.

Assign someone to create the copy for the brochure or engage an outside resource before giving the copy to the person "laying out" your brochure. Let that person know such things as:

- The profile of your targeted prospect
- The messages and the images that you want the brochure to express

You can find many capable of laying out your first company brochure at a very reasonable price by going to the internet. The layout person needs to know whether the brochure is to be printed by someone downloading it from your website or whether you intend to mail or hand it out in person

KEY POINT: Your first brochure doesn't have to be perfect to be effective. Most companies make changes to their brochures periodically.

When you are ready to have the brochure designed, tell the person who is creating the brochure such things as whether:

- The appearance of your brochure should be consistent with your company letterhead, envelopes, and business cards.
- You would like messages used in the brochures or websites of your competition to be paraphrased for use in your brochure
- Your budget guidelines for the brochure

Media Relations

You need a media relations strategy that has the goal of generating free publicity for your new business. Each media release should identify your company spokesperson, who should be contacted for interviews. The releases should also give the contact information for reaching the spokesperson.

There is a lot of potential free publicity generated by sending out media releases about your new company, and pointing out unique factors about you or your business, to all your local media, which announce the start of your business.

Other media releases should include announcements of each management-level person you hire and pictures of them.

KEY POINT: If you don't hear anything from the media within one week of your releases being sent, do follow-up phone calls.

Grand Opening Marketing

You will need a marketing budget for your Grand Opening and a plan for how the budget will be spent. Your budget will be impacted positively if your major suppliers provide marketing money to your business to promote the Grand Opening. Ask your suppliers for such help and use the argument that it will generate more sales of their products. You will not know if you can get the money unless you ask for the money.

You may want to offer special grand-opening pricing, unique guarantees, or other special terms, such as a money-back guarantee for those who buy a product or service during some Grand Opening period.

Next, develop your Grand Opening advertising messages for bringing about the objectives of:

- Create a desire for customers or clients to check out your products or services
- Provide name recognition for your new business
- Promote what is unique about your new company, product, or service compared to your competition for such things. These things could involve such

things as lower prices, better selection, or better service

When I launched TAB, I used the following message, "TAB is the affordable alternative to a high price board of directors."

KEY POINT: Don't run down your competition in your marketing messaging.

Strategic Plan #5: Hiring and On-Boarding Employees Before Grand Opening

If you want to start a "one-person show" business with no employees, you might want to skip this plan. But before you move on, consider that if you dream of a growing business, it's hard to do it as a one-person show because no one can do everything well in a start-up.

Hiring the first employees of a start-up business is often very challenging for new business owners. But who you hire as your first employees and how you onboard them will be crucial to the successful start of your business. This plan will help you to develop a strategic plan for hiring and onboarding employees before your business opens for business.

KEY POINT: Your strategic plan should serve as a roadmap for how you should be hiring and onboarding your initial employees.

Now I will share with you the ten-step approach I used when hiring and onboarding the first employees of TAB. The same steps have since been used successfully to hire and onboard employees by many start-ups.

Step #1: Decide What Employees are Needed

Determine what employees are needed to get your business ready for customers or clients and how many employees you need to handle the activities you need to be working on when you open for business.

Step #2: Job Descriptions

Write job descriptions for the positions you need to fill with each job description, including such things as:

- The position or title
- Name and title of the person to whom the employee will report and who will be reporting to the employee
- An overview of the tasks the employee will be responsible for doing with designation of what are daily, weekly or recurring activities

- A statement that the job description is not intended to be all-inclusive and the employee will also be expected to perform other reasonably related business duties if requested to do so by the person to whom the employee reports
- A statement that the job description is not a written or implied contract

Step #3: Employee Handbook

Next, create a small and straightforward employee handbook, or at least a file, that shares vital information every employee needs to know. You can find templates on the internet for you to use for creating your handbook.

After finishing your employee handbook, it is best to engage a labor law attorney to review it to be sure there is nothing in it that can be used against you in a lawsuit brought by an employee.

Step #4: Compensation of Employees

Decide on the compensation you will pay each of your new employees. Use the internet to research what others in your area are paying employees for comparable positions. You might also want to contact local employment agencies and ask what to pay employees for positions you are looking to fill.

Don't look just at the base salary. Try to find out typical incentives in compensation packages, such as bonuses or profit-sharing for managers and commissions based on sales results for salespeople.

Step #5: Onboarding Process

Know your onboarding process, including orientation sessions and pre-opening training your employees will receive.

Step #6: Protocols and Organizational Chart

Create whatever protocols and materials your new employees need to use when they start work. For example, a new salesperson will need a sales manual or a selling plan.

Your Organizational Chart should show the lines of authority in your business or, as some might see it, depict the hierarchy within your company.

Step #7: Recruiting Initial Employees

Develop a strategy for how you will attract employee applicants. What will your messages be, and how will you get the messages in front of potential applicants? You will need to decide which of the many websites you want to use that reach the type of employees you are recruiting.

Step #8: Interviewing Employee Applicants

You need an agenda for conducting job interviews with employee applicants and a philosophy for how you will conduct job interviews. Remember that the interview needs to be more than about you learning about your new applicant. The applicant is also learning about you and the company.

Allow yourself time before each interview to review the application of the applicant you will be meeting. Be set up to make notes on your observations during the interviews,

When the meeting starts, cover each of the items you have identified in an agenda for the meetings. The agenda should include such things as:

- The time allocated for the meeting
- A brief overview of what types of services or products your company will provide
- Hand the applicants a copy of your company's written long-term vision statement, and then discuss your vision for what you want the company to be like five to ten years into the future. Your vision for your company will influence some applicants. This can be a great selling point when recruiting employees for a start-up business.
- Address the elephant in the room about your company being a start-up and be transparent with applicants about the challenges of your business

being a start-up. Answer the concerns some applicants might have about taking a job with a start-up business since start-ups have no track record and, statistically speaking, have a high level of failure. Mention the possible benefit to them of the first employees in start-up positions being in a good position for future opportunities with the company. Explain that working for a start-up may be more enjoyable because employees can look at things with fresh and new perspectives and be flexible in handling situations.

- Hand out a copy of the job description for the applicant to review and then answer any questions about the job that the applicant may have

- Discuss the compensation for the job and employee benefits

- Talk about the person to whom the employee will be reporting and also those who will be reporting to the employee

- Hand applicants a copy of your company's written statement of culture and values, showing them the environment you desire for the start-up company. Explain the culture you want for your new business, and then ask the job candidates to share their views on the desired culture and values. Your statement will attract some prospects and have the opposite effect on others who are not attracted to the type of culture or values you want for your business.

Make it clear to the applicants that they must embrace the culture and values to become company employees. They will need to walk the talk of the desired culture and values, even when faced with challenging and stressful situations. For example, when hiring the first employees of TAB, I let each know that I only wanted to hire employees who would stay true to a company culture based on integrity, truthfulness, ethical actions, honesty, positivity, innovation, and work-life harmony. I explained that a byproduct of working for a company with this type of culture and values is that they will be proud that they work for the company.

- Discuss your company's non-compete and confidentiality policy, if you have one
- Share your philosophy about some things that will be meaningful to your employees. For example, when I started TAB, I shared that I wanted employees who would question how things are being done in the start-up business. I told the applicants that I wanted employees who could adapt and change how they are doing things based on what's being experienced.
- Question-and-answer session. Leave time at the end of the meeting for a question-and-answer time,

during which you should work to clear up any gray areas relating to the job

KEY POINT: After each interview and while it is fresh in your mind, edit the notes you took during the interview and identify any additional information you will need.

Step #9: Decide Who to Offer the Jobs

You will typically have to weigh many things when deciding who seems to have the best skills and behavior to fit your company's needs. So, be patient with the hiring process, and don't mistake relying on a "gut" instinct when deciding who you offer jobs to.

Before offering a job to an applicant, check the applicant's resume for "Red Flags," such as working for many companies and not staying more than a few years at each job.

Be sure to contact references. You may be surprised at material misrepresentations by the applicant.

Since your business is a start-up, give weight to applicants who have experience because they will need less training to do what is necessary for their jobs. Also, consider using one of the many inexpensive skill set tests and behavioral surveys to help you decide to whom you should offer a job.

KEY POINT: Don't hire someone just because you like the person. If the applicant does not have the needed skills or experience, you need to pass on the person. As the saying goes, "don't try to teach a pig to sing because it wastes your time and annoys the pig."

One last suggestion to consider before you offer someone a job. Ask yourself, "Would I enjoy working with the person?" Exceptional skills but the wrong personality can cause a nightmare for you and your other employees.

Step #10: Onboarding New Initial Employees

In addition to training new employees to do what they need to do in their jobs, you need one or more orientation meetings for all new employees. Your orientation meeting agenda should include such things as:

- A discussion of employee benefits, work hours, procedures for handling employee complaints, and discipline policy
- A discussion of your start-up company's service philosophy, including such things as customer

satisfaction philosophy, your policy for returned products, your policy for handling complaints, any price guarantee, or any money-back guarantee you may have if a customer or client is not satisfied with your products or services

- If you have one, review essential parts of your employee handbook. After the review and time for the new employees to read the handbook and ask questions, the new employees need to sign acknowledgments that they have read and accept the terms of the handbook and the confidentiality policy

- An overview of the training program that will be provided to them by the company

Before leaving hiring and onboarding, I want to add a suggestion that reflects a very true saying: "Be slow to hire and fast to fire." Sticking with a hiring mistake is costly. If you realize such a mistake has occurred, let the employee go, so you don't have to deal with the person during your company's Grand Opening. Also, if you terminate the employee, you won't have to be concerned that accepting that employee's bad work behavior will set an example for the conduct of your other employees.

Conclusion

You now know how to create up to five pre-opening strategic plans for what you need to do before starting your business from scratch. Each of them needs to have a goal, conceptual strategies for achieving the goal, and written action plans that identify, among other things, the required tasks to be completed before opening for business.

But even with the best pre-opening strategic plans, you will likely have failures and mistakes to address before opening your new business. So, manage your expectations. Don't keep doing what you thought would work that isn't working. Commit to adapting and making the changes needed for your pre-opening strategic plans to succeed, even if it requires significant adjustments. Just keep trying to find new and better ways to do things.

PART EIGHT: OUTSIDE RESOURCES

If you are like the founders of most start-ups, you will need to get funding from an outside resource and the money you can put into your new business. In Chapter Fifteen, I will share with you things you need to know to get the financing you need for your start-up business.

It is so crucial that you use your money wisely during the pre-opening phase of your start-up. One way to do this is to explore whether there are other outside resources that you should be using during this period. In Chapter Sixteen, I will discuss some of the most common outside resources that start-up businesses commonly engage in during the pre-opening phase.

CHAPTER FIFTEEN: FINANCING RESOURCES

Introduction

By now, you're excited about kickstarting your new business (or I sure hope so). But, if you are like most business founders, you realize that in addition to the money you can personally put into the business, you will need financing for the business from resources in addition to what you are personally able to put into the business.

Trust me; you don't want to be someone who started a business that failed because you moved ahead with starting an undercapitalized business. So, before you commit to starting the business, you need to know if you can arrange for the necessary funding to start and operate the business until it has a positive cash flow.

It isn't easy for start-ups to get the financing they need, particularly in the case of businesses starting from scratch, because there are many unknowns when starting from scratch and a high risk of failure. But the odds of getting the financing you need increase significantly if you do it correctly, and it starts with you recognizing that getting funding is a high-level priority.

This chapter will show you how to identify what your business will need, what you can put into your business, and what to do to bring about your best chances of getting the funding your business will need.

So, let's look at the first step, which is identifying the amount of financing your business will need.

Step One: Amount of Financing Needed

The first step is to project the amount of money your business will need for which you will need to get financing. This is the amount your business will need until it has positive cash flow, less the amount of money you will be able to provide to your business.

How Much Money Will Your New Company Need?

Some founders can financially bootstrap all the money their start-ups need without needing to borrow anything from outside sources. Kudos to them, but most new businesses need additional funds beyond what their founders can provide out of their assets.

To identify how much additional funds your business will need, you need to first conservatively project how much money your new company will need before it reaches a point of positive cash flow. Very few new businesses start to make money immediately, and being strapped for cash can have severe consequences when things don't go as planned.

Businesses can rapidly find themselves in trouble if they need to operate while under-capitalized. So you must have access to the money necessary to start and then carry your new business until it has reached a positive cash flow.

Of course, identifying the amount of money needed for your new business is much easier if you are buying a franchise to start your business. This is because the franchisor and current franchisees will have information to share with you based on the experience of other franchisees.

In contrast, when you start your business from scratch, there are many more unknowns, which makes it much harder to do your estimations of the money your business will need. But despite this, you must do your cash flow estimate with a view of how much money the business would need to weather a worst-case or almost worst-case situation.

Your cash flow projections will need to include sales forecasts. One of the challenges is that it's tough to predict sales results when starting a business from scratch. So, offer your best estimates of future sales, but do the sales forecast with **No** "puffing." Be conservative. Your cash flow projection should not overestimate what your business will accomplish. Instead, the projection should reflect what sales revenue would look like if sales turn out to be lower than what you optimistically think they should be.

Next, conservatively project all costs to get your business to when it is experiencing a positive cash flow.

Your cash flow projection should include estimated costs for all foreseeable expenses. Include a "cushion" for expenses you can't foresee and costs that could be higher than expected to help your new business have adequate money resources if the costs are higher.

When doing your cash flow project, you will need to assume some things if your business will be borrowing money. Assumptions of interest rate, principal amortization, and how long you will have to repay loans will affect the cash flow projection.

Many assets, such as computer systems equipment, can be leased instead of bought. This can have the effect of reducing the amount of money that the business needs to borrow. Leasing assets will generally keep more money in your business during the time it builds toward positive cash flow compared to buying assets. So, when making your cash flow projection, reflect the cash flow based upon leasing, rather than buying, assets the business will need.

You will, of course, have to decide who will create the cash flow analysis. Will it be you or one of your employees? If so, the good news is that inexpensive software is available to help you prepare your cash flow projections. You might want an accountant to review the forecast if you're doing it yourself or with a non-accountant employee. You may, as an alternative, consider engaging an accountant to prepare the needed cash flow analysis.

How Much Money Will You Invest in Your Company?

Next, consider how much money you can invest in your company from your personal sources. Consider your available cash and liquid assets, such as your stocks, bonds, and other securities. In addition, consider things you can and are willing to borrow against, such as your home or other real estate you own, your insurance policies, and your credit card lines.

When considering how much of your assets to put into your business, include the income you'll need to live on until the business can provide the income you need.

KEY POINT: To determine the additional funds your new business will need, just deduct the amount of money you will put into the business from the total amount the business needs. For example, if you project that your new business will need $100,000, you can put in $60,000. You need $40,000 in additional financing.

Step Two: Potential Money Sources

Although getting financing for start-ups is challenging, your chances of getting the money you need go up significantly if you have the correct money source for your situation.

Let's look at some of the funding sources that you should consider.

Friends and Relatives

Many have generated the money needed for their new businesses through loans or investments from friends or relatives. Often the money was lent or invested based on friendship or relationship rather than an analysis of business facts. However, there is a big downside to this approach. Your relationship with friends or relatives who put money into your business will probably be damaged if your start-up business fails and they don't get all their money back.

Government Agencies That Provide Grants or Guarantee Loans

Most countries have government programs that help finance small and midsize start-ups because of the value, such as employment, such businesses bring to the countries. Sometimes the help is with grants.

Often, the help involves programs in which a government agency guarantees lenders, who are certified to participate in the program, as much as 90% of any amounts they may lose due to lending to start-up businesses. As a result of the low risk to the lender, the lenders make loans to start-ups that would not otherwise be made.

Use the internet to research government programs that apply to the type of business you want to start and see if you might qualify for the help.

Banks

Many banks are skittish about lending to a start-up business unless they get a government guarantee to remove most of the risk of loan default. Also, banks that will lend to start-up businesses generally require the founders to "put it all on the line" with personal guarantees and may require the pledging of assets of the founder as collateral. Such assets include savings, stocks, bonds, pensions, and personal property. When assets are being used as collateral for loans, the banks may require appraisals for assets.

Lending Institutions Other Than Banks

In some countries, institutions other than banks are lenders for start-up businesses. For example, in the USA, there are Savings and Loan organizations. An easy check on the internet will let you know if any such non-bank institutional lenders exist in your country.

Investors

Individual investors(s) and Venture Capital fund investors are generally not interested in financing small to midsize business start-ups. An exception to this general rule is when there is potential for a substantial return on investment. You can start your search on the internet looking for an investor for the amount of money you are hoping to raise from investors.

Investors in such start-ups have in common that an important factor they will consider is whether they believe that you, the person leading the start-up business, are someone they believe in.

But significant differences in investors' objectives impact whether particular investors are good fits for you. Let's look at some of these differences:

- The range of money the investor likes to invest in any individual company. For example, some investors are only interested in investing an amount within a specific range in any one business, such as $500,000 to $5,000,000. Some limit their investment in any individual start-up business to no more than $100,000.

- The amount of ownership they expect for their investment

- The control or involvement factor they expect in return for an investment of a specific amount. Some investors expect to control. Some investors want to invest only if they can be "involved investors." One way this is done is for the investor to place one or more people in management positions within the company. Others are passive investors.

- The industries in which the investors want to make their investments. Some, for example, limit their start-up business investments to technology-based start-ups.
- The expected return on investment
- How long do they prefer to keep their investment in the business before they sell their interest?

If you are looking for an investor rather than a lender, things are much more complex for getting the money you want. You should consider engaging someone who specializes in helping businesses get money from investors.

Franchisor Financing

If you are buying a franchise to start a business, the franchisor might help your financing needs by:

- Financing a portion of the franchise fees and training fees
- Providing loan guarantees so you can get loans for the business
- Leasing equipment you need to operate the business

Accounts Receivable Lenders

Some companies will commit to lending money to the start-up business for a line of credit based on a percentage of the sound current accounts receivables the business generates. The accounts receivable lenders require security because the borrowing company pledges its accounts receivables as security. The credit line may be for as much as 80 percent of the start-up company's good current outstanding receivables.

Guarantees and Consignment From Key Suppliers

If suppliers believe that a new business will buy a lot of goods from a start-up business, they may be willing to help the start-up in such different ways as the following:

- Giving long terms for the payment for the initial order the new business buys from the suppliers
- Consigning products to the new businesses, so payment for the products does not need to be made until the start-up business sells the products
- Guaranteeing loans or lines of credit for institutions to lend money to the businesses

Current Employer

If you want to start a business, your current employer may provide loans or guarantee loans to help finance your start-up business. This can happen if your employer strongly believes in your ability to make the new business a success and if one or both of the two following situations exist:

- Your current employer sees a significant help your new business will be to the current employer's business. For example, the new business might become a supplier to the current employers with attractive terms.

- You offer your current employer part ownership in your new business. For example, one employer-provided loan to help some of her managers start new businesses in return for 49 percent ownership of the start-up companies.

Service Contracts and Prepaid Subscriptions

You might consider setting up a program for your customers or clients to buy service contracts or prepaid subscriptions. The following are examples:

- New gyms had sold discounted memberships, which were paid in advance before the gyms opened

- Customer electronics or appliance stores sell service contracts for the repair of items if they should fail in the future

- Newsletters selling subscriptions to receive the newsletter in the future

Step #3: Creating an Information Package for Lender/Investor

Creating an information package to send to your potential money sources before they meet with you is hard work but very important. You want your package to prime the pump for interest in financing your business. So, invest the time needed to develop the best presentation package you can create.

There is another benefit to going through the process of creating the package. Doing it will force you to think through things and challenge them as you put them into the package. If you are like most start-up founders, you will recognize and eliminate mistakes when creating the package.

Your objective is for money sources to get the package, to see things in it that will help them decide to put money into your start-up. So, your information package needs to be compelling as to why it would be wise to provide your start-up with funding.

KEY POINT: Keep your package to no more than 2000 words long — unless your new business has a lot of complexity.

Now, let's look at the things that should be in a clear, concise, and very easily readable informational package:

Company Story. Include a short general description of your new business. It should include what you expect your product or service mix to be. Explain what you see as the demand for the products or services you will be offering.

Briefly explain how you will market and sell your product or service, such as your strategy for advertising, media relations, or plans to attend trade shows.

If your business sells products, you should explain why your projected turn-on inventory is reasonable for the industry in which you will be operating. If your start-up company is selling services, explain what the services are. Then provide a brief explanation of why you believe there is a demand for the services you plan to sell.

Your company story should refer to any demand trend for your product or service that you can back up with research, such as an article from a trade magazine about the future of the industry in which your company will be operating.

Current and Potential Competition. Identify companies you believe will be your primary competition. Then explain why you think you'll be able to compete against the other businesses. For example, explain why you believe you have an edge if you believe your product or service has an advantage over the established competition.

Financing Amount. Show the amount of money you will be putting into the business. Then show the amount of financing your start-up business needs from sources other than you.

Financial Projections. Include financial projections for profit and loss statements and cash flow analysis. A lender will look at your profit, loss, and cash flow projections to see how you expect to repay a loan. Most lenders will want your forecasts to include at least the first, second, and third years of operation.

Your projection of expenses should be in line with the average expense ratios for your industry. If a money source believes that your forecasts do not include all the costs you are likely to have, you will lose credibility. So be sure to include all the expenses you anticipate looking ahead.

Your Profile. You will be responsible for making the start-up business successful; therefore, you want to show that you have the skills to lead the business successfully. So, include a summary of your business experience with highlights of business things you have accomplished

Statement of Your Assets and Liabilities of Borrowing Money. Loans to start-up businesses typically require founders to guarantee that loans will be repaid personally. So lenders will be interested in your assets and liabilities. You can be proactive by providing your personal financial statement in the informational package and pointing out any assets you are open to using as collateral for the loan. If you have appraisals of any valuable assets you are offering to pledge, you might want to include them.

Company Personnel at Time of Launch. Mention the roles of managers you will employ when opening the doors for business, along with an overview of other employees you plan to hire. If your business launches with layers of employees, you might also include an organizational chart.

Company Location. Mention the type of location you want for your business, which might include the location's demographics that will be important to your business. If you have a particular location in mind for where your business will operate, share what will be the rent or mortgage payments, utilities, etc., that you will have to pay for the space.

Technology. Include any significant technology you plan to use in your business.

KEY POINT: An information package that might intrigue venture capitalists differs from one seeking to interest a bank.

After completing the information package, send a copy to your prospective funding resources at least a week before meeting with them.

Step Four: Preparing for Meetings with Money Sources

Preparation is key to successful meetings with money sources. The following are things to do when preparing for the meetings:

- **Create things that you will use or hand out at the meeting.** For example, you should create a pitch deck to use at the meetings that should have no more than 25 well-designed slides. The slides will help you cover the key points you need to cover, including the following six "C" factors:

character, capacity, collateral, capital, conditions, and credit score.

- **Learn the meaning of terms likely to be used during your meetings with money sources.** Few things will make you look as bad with a lender or investor as when you do not understand the financial terms they use at your meetings. So, be sure you understand standard terms that lenders and investors may use, such as assets, liabilities, equity, debits, credits, gross profit, and net profit.

- **Practice Answering Commonly Asked Questions.** Discuss with your accountant what questions are likely to be asked by experienced lending or investing professionals and how you should answer the questions. The following are typical examples of questions:

  o How did you create your cash flow projection? Your answers should show that you understand the cash flow projections developed for your new business.

  o Why do you feel the sales forecasts and the costs you project for developing and producing them are reasonable.?

  o Do you have a good credit rating? Several inexpensive sources can provide a copy of your credit rating, which reflects your credit history over recent years. Lenders and investors will check out your credit rating before they provide lending or invest in your business. So, if you have a poor credit history, it is better to address it proactively and have an explanation ready for why you have a poor credit rating.

o Are there any unusual things about your business that we should know? For example, if your business will be exporting products, you should be prepared to discuss how your business will handle currency fluctuations.

Step Five: Meeting with Money Sources

When you meet with any potential lender or investor, make sure you have to have your selling hat on. After all, you're pitching more than just what your business can do: Selling them to *you and your new business!*

Sell your story by focusing on key points you need to emphasize for the money source. For example, explain why you anticipate the sales you expect.

When money resources ask questions, keep your answers as straightforward and concise as possible. Don't try to fake it if you don't know the answer. If you are not confident that you can answer the questions well, consider engaging someone to help you answer questions.

KEY POINT: Don't say something during the meeting that conflicts with your package.

Step Six: After Meeting Money Source

There are two possible outcomes from your meeting. One is that the money source says yes to your money request. Hooray! Game over, right? Not quite, because now you have to negotiate the best terms you can get from the source. So, sharpen your business financing negotiating techniques before sitting down with a funding source that has said yes to your request.

The other outcome is that the money source says no and rejects your funding application. If this happens, try to find out why. Knowing the reason will help you to decide whether to persist in trying to break through in a different way with the party who said no.

One reason start-up business loans are turned down is because of the unwillingness of the founder to be personally liable for the repayment of any loans for the business that the business does not pay back. If this is the reason, is there openness to providing a guarantee? If so, you can go back to the party who said no with the changed approach toward guaranteeing the loan.

The no response might be because of the un unwilling of the founder to put assets at risk if things go wrong in the start-up business you want to start. If this is important for a

253

comfort level with the financial risk you need, you may decide not to change your position and pass on starting the business.

Or you may decide that receiving a "no" from one source should not deter your fundraising efforts to try to get a "yes" from another money source. Instead, you may use the information you received from the naysayer to change your financing strategy or to repackage your request to make it more acceptable to other money sources. You may find that money is available somewhere else with a revised strategy or presentation.

Conclusion

If you are like most business founders, you will need financing beyond what you can invest in your new business before you can commit to starting the business you want to start. Follow the steps in this chapter, and your chances of getting your business's money will significantly increase.

CHAPTER SIXTEEN: OTHER OUTSIDE RESOURCES

Challenge yourself as to whether the number of employees you are thinking of hiring for your small or midsize business could be reduced by engaging outside resources. When most companies start, they cannot afford to hire all the employees needed to provide the start-up's services.

Let's look at the following outside services that all start-up businesses should consider engaging and other outside services that should be considered as an alternative to hiring employees, at least in the start-up and early stage of the business.

Attorney and Certified/Chartered Accountant

In general, small and midsize start-ups don't employ a full-time attorney or a certified/chartered accountant because they do not need them full-time and because of the expense. But, they do need the services of an attorney or accountant.

The attorney or your certified/chartered accountant you use will help you to choose the right business type of legal entity for your new business and also ensure that your new business complies with legal requirements for that type of entity

An attorney will do such things for your start-up business as:

- Register your business name and a trademark that you may want to use
- Review your employee manual,
- Review legal documents before signing them, such as leases, franchise agreements, bank agreements, employee confidentiality agreements, and license agreements
- Create the needed corporation shareholders or board of directors minutes if your new business is incorporated
- Conduct a patent search to learn if a product has been patented and, if not, apply for you to have the rights to the patent

An accountant can do such things as:

- Preparing payroll tax reports
- Profit and loss statements
- Financial projections
- Break-even analysis
- Audits

Even if you hire a full-time bookkeeper, most bookkeepers cannot do some of these things.

Engaging the Wrong Attorney or Accountant Can be Costly

If you are wondering how to find the right attorney and certified/chartered accountant for your needs, there is a wrong and best way. The wrong way is to engage an attorney or accountant because you know them socially or like how they look on TV.

The best way is to get recommendations from someone who has used the professionals. Ask your banker, other business owners you know, and colleagues in trade associations or buying groups you have joined for recommendations. If you can't get a recommendation, you can use the internet to find websites of such professionals in your area.

For many start-ups, engaging an attorney or accountant who works from home may provide qualified work at a lower price than a firm. Many attorneys and accountants have left firms to work remotely for themselves out of their homes to have more freedom and flexibility in their work/life balance.

Concerning what to look for in an attorney, give importance to the attorney having business law experience. An attorney may be brilliant in non-business legal matters, such as accident lawsuits, but would have a big learning curve to do good work for you in business law matters.

Concerning what to look for in an accountant, there is a significant advantage in engaging someone certified/chartered. Many suppliers, lenders, and investors have respect and confidence in their statements that they do not have with statements from accountants who are not certified or chartered.

When you have narrowed it down to a small number of the attorneys and accountants you want to check out, go to their websites. Their websites should provide information about their experience in your business field or industry. The more attorneys and accountants who understand your business field or industry, the less time you spend on a learning curb, and this should mean less cost for you.

The websites may also list certifications in particular areas that are meaningful to you.

If satisfied with what you see on the websites, call the attorneys or certified/chartered accountants and ask for free interview meetings conducted either virtually or in person. Some may agree to free interview meetings, and others will want to charge for their time.

During the meeting, ask such questions as:

- What is a reasonable time to expect a return call?

- Do you require a retainer?

- What is your minimum billing time unit, such as five minutes or 15 minutes?

- What are their rates for specific services provided? If your start-up is like most small and midsize start-ups, the rates will be very important to you. But don't try to negotiate rates during your interview meeting.

- How long would their quoted fees be in place? This is important because you don't want a low-cost package offered to get you as a new client and then find the rates significantly increased in subsequent years.

- Is there any litigation in which the professional or firm is currently involved, and any recent litigation that was settled?

- Ask for client references, names, and contact information.

You may want to interview a few attorneys or accountants as part of your selection process before engaging the ones you want to use. Select your attorney and accountant, at least in part, based on whether you think that you would enjoy working with them.

KEY POINT: Once you have made a selection, there is nothing wrong with negotiating the fees charged.

Business Consultants

Business consultants are excellent sources of specialized business knowledge. However, from a practical standpoint, most start-up businesses can not afford to engage consultants before starting their businesses.

If you do engage a business consultant and the consultant will have access to your business-sensitive information, ask for the consultant to sign a confidentiality agreement.

Management Development Training

Management training programs are available from many different resources, which you might want for yourself or your managers. TAB's management development training programs include blended learning, a combination of online and virtual face-to-face training provided by a TAB implementer trainer.

Section Five: Independent Sales Representatives

Many businesses need people located away from the main offices for sales efforts. These people do not have to be employees. Your start-up business might be better off using independent sales representatives or manufacturers' agents as an alternative to hiring sales employees.

You might want to use independent sales representatives in the early stages of the business but replace them with full-time employed salespeople as your business grows, or you may decide to continue using independent sales representatives.

The percentage of sales they make is higher than the sales commission you would pay an employee. But, you have no payroll costs for them because sales representatives are paid on results. This gives you a predictable cost-to-sales ratio. For example, if you have a five percent arrangement, you know your sales expenses in that territory will be five percent without considering salary guarantees.

Sales representatives sell products or services for several clients within protected territories where they are the only ones selling your products or services.

Using sales representatives allows you to penetrate more markets faster and more efficiently because they often have a close relationship with buyers of different products or services from the sales representatives. Often the relationship between sales representatives and customers or clients can be of many years. The customers or clients may be very loyal to the sales representative. They will switch from your product if the sales representative stops representing your product or service and starts representing an alternative product or service.

Another disadvantage of using sales representatives is that many provide little to no training for those who buy your products or services.

You can find sales representatives to interview by finding out what sales representatives are currently selling other products that do not compete with your targeted customers or clients within the geographic territories you want to enter. For example, if you are manufacturing a line of sofas, you might want to engage a sales representative selling lamps to furniture stores.

Conclusion

Most start-ups have financial limitations that restrict the amount of expertise they have in the way of employees. Using outside resources can help keep costs for start-up businesses in line while providing the services help needed.

CONCLUSION

By now, you know if starting a business is a good fit for you. Starting a business that becomes successful is fulfilling and enjoyable. But, it can be anything but pleasant if the business is a failure. Hopefully, after reading this book, you know what you need to do to achieve your dream of starting a successful business.

It takes self-discipline to keep yourself accountable for doing what you must accomplish to start your new business. There will be times when things don't go how you thought they would. Expect there to be obstacles in your pathway to starting your business. But, view these obstacles as challenges that you will overcome. Don't let them stop you from launching your new business.

Once you launch your new business, get ready to take the baton of knowledge from other business owners. Once your business has started, you may be eligible to become a TAB Peer Accelerator Board member. Membership in these boards, which can be virtual or in-person, is for founders of businesses during the early years they are in business.

Peer Accelerator Board membership will provide affordable non-theoretical advice to help you address 75-90% of the challenges that stand in the way of your business's success. You can learn more about the TAB Accelerator Board program by going to TABBoards.com.